Angel Numbers 1-9 Meaning

How to Understand the Messages Angels Are Showing You for Twin Flames, Love, Grief, Lost Loved Ones, Change, and Friends

Dawn Hazel

© Copyright 2022 - All rights reserved.

The content contained within this book may not be reproduced, duplicated or transmitted without direct written permission from the author or the publisher.

Under no circumstances will any blame or legal responsibility be held against the publisher, or author, for any damages, reparation, or monetary loss due to the information contained within this book, either directly or indirectly.

Legal Notice:

This book is copyright protected. It is only for personal use. You cannot amend, distribute, sell, use, quote or paraphrase any part, or the content within this book, without the consent of the author or publisher.

Disclaimer Notice:

Please note the information contained within this document is for educational and entertainment purposes only. All effort has been executed to present accurate, up to date, reliable, complete information. No warranties of any kind are declared or implied. Readers acknowledge that the author is not engaged in the rendering of legal, financial, medical or professional advice. The content within this book has been derived from various sources. Please consult a licensed professional before attempting any techniques outlined in this book.

By reading this document, the reader agrees that under no circumstances is the author responsible for any losses, direct or indirect, that are incurred as a result of the use of the information contained within this document, including, but not limited to, errors, omissions, or inaccuracies.

Table of Contents

INTRODUCTION 1
   HAVE YOU BEEN NOTICING THE SAME NUMBERS APPEARING REPEATEDLY? 1
      About Dawn Hazel 2

CHAPTER 1: WHAT ARE ANGEL NUMBERS? 5
   ANGEL NUMBERS 5
   WHY DO ANGELS COMMUNICATE THIS WAY? 6
   THE NUMEROLOGY CONNECTION 7
   HOW DO THESE NUMBERS WORK? 8
   WHAT DOES IT MEAN IF I SEE DIFFERENT ANGEL NUMBERS WITHIN MINUTES OF EACH OTHER? 9

CHAPTER 2: ANGEL NUMBERS FOR LOVE 12
   TWOS 12
      2 .... *13*
      22 .... *13*
      222 .... *14*
      2222 .... *14*
      3 .... *15*
      33 .... *15*
      6 .... *16*
      60 .... *16*
      64 .... *17*
      6666 .... *17*
      808 .... *18*
   OTHER ANGEL NUMBERS WITH LOVE MESSAGES 18

IF YOU HAVEN'T FOUND YOUR ANGEL NUMBER MESSAGE HERE, CORE NUMBER TWO SPROUTS MORE ANGEL MESSAGES RELATED TO LOVE AND PARTNERSHIPS. CHAPTER 3: ANGEL NUMBERS AND MESSAGES FOR TWIN FLAMES 23
   ONES AND ELEVENS 25
      1010 .... *25*
      11 .... *25*
      111 .... *26*
      1101 .... *26*
      1111 .... *27*

1122	27
1212	27
2	28
22	28
222	28
2121	29
2222	29
33	30
333	30
444	30
6999	31
8	31
88	31
Other Angel Numbers for Twin Flames	32

CHAPTER 4: ANGEL NUMBERS FOR GRIEF AND LOST LOVED ONES ... 36

Angel Numbers for Those in Grief ... 36

44	36
222	36
333	37
555	37
666	37
777	37
888	38
999	38
1221	40

Angel Numbers for Lost Loved Ones ... 40

222	40
333	40
444	40
888	41
922	42
1212	43

CHAPTER 5: ANGEL NUMBERS ABOUT CHANGE ... 44

How Angels Signal a Change Coming Into Your Life ... 44

00	45
1	45
3	46
5	46
9	47
22	49
123	50
555	50

  919..51
  1010...*51*
 OTHER ANGEL NUMBERS INDICATING COMING CHANGES 51

CHAPTER 6: ANGEL NUMBERS REGARDING FRIENDS AND FRIENDSHIPS 52
 WHY ANGELS SEND YOU MESSAGES ABOUT FRIENDS AND FRIENDSHIPS........................52
  111..*53*
  211...*54*
  212...*54*
  414...*54*
  616...*55*
  777...*55*
 OTHER ANGEL NUMBERS WITH FRIENDSHIP MESSAGES *56*

CHAPTER 7: ANGEL NUMBERS WITH RECURRING ONES 59
 CORE NUMBER ONE 59
  11...*60*
  111...*61*
  1111...*62*

CHAPTER 8: ANGEL NUMBERS WITH RECURRING TWOS 63
 CORE NUMBER TWO 63
  22...*65*
  222...*66*
  2222...*66*

CHAPTER 9: ANGEL NUMBERS WITH RECURRING THREES 69
 CORE NUMBER THREE 69
  33...*70*
  333...*72*
  3333...*72*

CHAPTER 10: ANGEL NUMBERS WITH RECURRING FOURS 75
 CORE NUMBER FOUR 75
  44...*76*
  444...*78*
  4444...*79*

CHAPTER 11: ANGEL NUMBERS WITH RECURRING FIVES 81
 CORE NUMBER FIVE 81
  55...*82*
  555...*83*
  5555...*84*

CHAPTER 12: ANGEL NUMBERS WITH RECURRING SIXES 87

CORE NUMBER SIX 87
- *66* *88*
- *666* *89*
- *6666* *90*

CHAPTER 13: ANGEL NUMBERS WITH RECURRING SEVENS 93

CORE NUMBER SEVEN 93
- *77* *94*
- *777* *96*
- *7777* *97*

CHAPTER 14: ANGEL NUMBERS WITH RECURRING EIGHTS 99

CORE NUMBER EIGHT 99
- *88* *100*
- *888* *101*
- *8888* *102*

CHAPTER 15: ANGEL NUMBERS WITH RECURRING NINES 105

CORE NUMBER NINES 105
- *99* *106*
- *999* *107*
- *9999* *108*

CHAPTER 16: ANGEL NUMBERS WITH RECURRING ZEROS 109

CORE NUMBER ZERO 109
- *00* *110*
- *000* *111*
- *0000* *113*

CHAPTER 17: GREATLY SIGNIFICANT ANGEL NUMBERS 115

- *1000 (10:00)* *115*
- *1010 (10:10)* *115*
- *1111 (11:11)* *116*
- *1122 (11:22)* *116*
- *1222 (12:22)* *116*
- *13* *117*
- *1313 (13:13)* *117*
- *1414 (14:14)* *118*
- *1515 (15:15)* *118*
- *1616 (16:16)* *119*
- *1618 (16:18)* *119*
- *1707 (17:07)* *119*

1717 (17:17) *119*
1808 (18:08) *120*
1818 (18:18) *120*
1919 (19:19) *121*
1333 (13:33) *121*
1555 (15:55) *121*
1999 .... *122*
2020 (20:20) *122*
2112 (21:12) *123*
2121 (21:21) *123*
2222 (22:22) *123*
2999 .... *124*
303 (3:03) *124*
321 .... *126*
3999 .... *126*
404 .... *127*
4999 .... *128*
5999 .... *128*
618 (6:18) *129*
6220 .... *130*
6999 .... *130*
707 (7:07) *131*
777 .... *131*
7999 .... *131*
808 .... *132*
888 .... *132*
8585 .... *134*
8999 .... *134*

CONCLUSION **135**

WHAT IT MEANS IF YOU STOP SEEING ANGEL NUMBERS 136
Keeping a Journal *137*

REFERENCES **141**

Images *145*

Introduction

Life is tough enough without having more numbers thrown at you, yet some numbers appear to help you through a situation instead of causing you stress. For years, we've been calling these random-seeming numbers that seep into our consciousness and suggest a deeper meaning "angel numbers."

You may have noticed if you are asking for divine help, are manifesting, or are stressed over a decision, that you might see the same numbers over and over again. This is because when you're in need of direction or are looking for answers to questions, angels and guides often gift you messages and confirmation using everyday instances of digits and sequences of numbers. These numerical sequences often contain special messages and comfort for you.

If you've ever wondered about angel numbers, where and how people receive them, and how you might decode them and receive their help yourself, read on.

Have You Been Noticing the Same Numbers Appearing Repeatedly?

We've all had periods when we may notice a number and feel it may hold a greater significance than just the address where we're attending an interview, or a flight or train we're about to board.

For example, you might see 12:12 on the clock twice in 24 hours if you're experiencing insomnia, but what made you look at the clock exactly twelve minutes past midnight? You may see 12:12 again within minutes if your computer clock and your TV or phone clocks aren't synchronized.

The next day, you might note that you receive several texts, all time-stamped 12:12, or your invoice from the store is also time-stamped 12:12. Driving along, you may be stuck behind a car with the license number including 1212, or you have to call a new number later that contains 1212.

While the first two instances may be coincidence, the appearance of 1212 in growing randomness reinforces that it's an angel number with a message for you. Angel numbers often repeat a digit—for example, 222—or a sequence such as 1144 or 1234.

You may be wondering if you need special abilities to delve into the meaning of angel messages or puzzle out their message. Absolutely not! Anyone can do it, and many people who read and find support through angel messengers are just like you and me.

Recognizing that a number may hold a message for you isn't that hard. In fact, you may find it harder to ignore angel numbers if your guides are trying their all to communicate with you. Decoding the number or sequence's meaning may be a little confusing, but it's not meant to be. All you need is a minute or two to look up the meaning and a nudge from your intuition. Using this book to decode and explore angel number messages is as simple as scrolling through the table of contents for the number. If your concern or current situation is linked to Love, Grief, or Changes, simply look for the number under those categories. Dedicated sections for Twin Flames and Lost Loved Ones are also included. Highly significant numbers can also be found under the digit's Core Number section or in Chapter 17.

The purpose of this book is to share encouragement, hope, solace, and inspiration by helping you decode and understand angel number messages.

About Dawn Hazel

For as long as I can remember, I've been reading the cards and keeping an eye on the numbers that the angels have been sending me and learning how to interpret the numerical messages during different stages and situations in my life. I've been lucky in that my family has always noticed and followed the advice of angel numbers and the tarot cards. Sometimes I might think of them as a short "weather forecast" when it comes to my spiritual journey.

I've been helping people through reading cards for over twenty years and studying angel numbers closely for over ten years. Angel numbers and intuition have saved my life twice. I love how they help bring greater clarity and focus to my readings and intuition. For the future, I'd like to see where the universe and the lessons sent are going to take me. I hope you'll join me in this journey signposted by our Angel Numbers and gain from it as much as I do.

Chapter 1:

What Are Angel Numbers?

How do you spot angel numbers and can you dial an angel number to get an angel's help? I've never tried it, but angel numbers are used by the angels to dial *you* in!

Recurring and repeating numbers appearing throughout the day or over a prolonged period of time are the main characteristics that set angel numbers apart from other random numbers you may note. Their appearance isn't meant to haunt you but to send you a gentle message. It's like a nudge from the angels saying, "Hey! We have some mail for you. Look up this number to receive your message!"

Angel Numbers

Using these numbers as coded messages, your guardians and spiritual advisors nudge you in the right direction and comfort you whenever you need or ask for their help. While we call these message numbers angel numbers, these spiritual dispatches and the guides who send them transcend religious affiliations and cultures. Angel numbers can be applied universally to anyone and are hidden in nature and mathematics everywhere! Take for example the golden ratio, also known as the divine proportion: 1.618 or *Phi*. As an angel number, you might recognize it as [1618](#), or [618](#). Examples of the golden ratio are found all over nature and the universe, from your face to the distances between the orbits of the planets. It's something that your mind and soul seek instinctively to find harmony. If you see these numbers often, your angels may be reminding you to include this ratio in your work, in aspects of your life, or to appreciate that much of creation has an underlying beauty and truth that they'd like you to explore now. They may suggest you take art lessons or experiment with baking using the ratio!

Angels don't usually send obtuse messages, so they reveal the numerical messages in ways that will be unmistakable to you. While many are familiar with three and four digit angel numbers such as 333 and 8888, angels can send you messages via any number: a bold 'one' popping out at you in store promotions, the counter that serves you, or the elevator being stuck for an inordinately long time on the first floor. Or maybe your appointment is at 2 p.m. in Room Two, on the 2nd floor, on 2 February. What an easy appointment to remember! And would it bring you a partnership, a second chance, or love—romantic or otherwise? That's between you and your angels. But if you'd rather not ponder over your angel message for too long, the answer to the question "which of these elements do you most need to bring balance to your life?" would be your hint as to your personal angel number message for that day regarding the recurring twos. And if you see recurring threes, that's likely another angel message regarding another aspect of your life!

Why Do Angels Communicate This Way?

The guides in your celestial team prefer a subtle approach and gentle reminders instead of shocking you with their appearance. History shows us that their materializing can sometimes cause greater harm than good to individuals. So, slipping in their messages unobtrusively prevents alarming you and upsetting those around you. In the hubbub of your day, a whisper or other verbal message may be missed or quickly forgotten. With us seeing and interacting with numbers throughout the day, digits provide the perfect way to send messages to everyone in the world, no matter who they are, where they live, or what their situation may be. Even more elegant in their simplicity, with numbers constantly around, it's fairly easy for your guides to remind you throughout the day of their message and continuing support.

With angel numbers, there's no fanfare or blaring of trumpet; no "ta da!" moment, although you may see your angel numbers lit up at night. It doesn't matter if you see the digits in your environment, dream the numbers in your sleep, doodle the sequence in a meeting, or hear the numbers called out on the radio. These all reinforce and carry the same message to you—a message you may have otherwise missed because you were too caught up in the demands of your everyday life.

The Numerology Connection

Numerology, like astrology, is the science of studying the influence and vibrations of the essence of numbers on a person. In other words, each number from zero to eleven, twenty-two, and thirty-three are all said to have a specific vibration and influence on a person, or hold hidden information pertaining to their life such as their Life Path, or Life's Challenges. Discovering the underlying numbers that govern your life or a situation reveals the influences and nature of yourself and how you approach situations. In a way, your numerology profile is like your background-running apps in life, exerting influences on what your life looks like—inside and outside!

Angel numbers most often build on numerology.

It's no wonder, then, that a popular way of decoding angel messages is by beginning with numerology. When a number with two, three or four digits appears, taking the meaning of the main numbers from the numerology system and interpreting the numbers individually, in groups, or by adding the sum of the numbers gives us the angel messages. Interpreting these messages in different contexts (love, twin flame, grief, friendship) gives us more personalized messages. Intuition also plays a part in angel number communication, more so than with numerology.

Learning the core number meanings from the numerology system is a great way to decipher and interpret angel numbers based on your intuition and current experiences. Find more information on core numbers, their numerological and their angelic number meanings in Chapter 7 through to Chapter 16 and begin decoding angel messages for yourself.

How Do These Numbers Work?

You may puzzle over whether you truly are receiving angelic guidance and not just envisioning and forcefully creating situations so you see what you wish to see—an angel number. Anyone who's tried this will admit that in their efforts to see 11:11 or 12:12 on the clock, the moment they looked, the digits rolled over to 11:12 or 12:13 or remained at 11:10 or 12:11. It just doesn't work because there has to be synchronicity and spiritual connection that can't be forced. The universe and your guides show you what you need to see in that moment of time. Sometimes, when you've looked up at the clock and noticed that it's 10:10 or 22:22, you may find that time tends to 'expand' the minute before the digits roll over and it takes much longer than expected for the minute to pass. This is confirmation that your experience and message isn't a fluke. The angels and guides will hold the number up to you until you consciously register and note it. Sometimes, they may send you more than a single number. You may receive a progressive sequence. For example, during the course of two days, you may see 09:09, 10:10. 12:12, 14:14 and 17:17 on the same days, though maybe not in that order. This could mean that your current life is accelerating to conclude a cycle or raise your frequency up before you begin a new growth cycle.

While numerology has set meanings to the numbers that may differ between its various systems, and many agree on the different angel numbers, often your own intuition and experience may modify or suggest to you a new or unique-to-you meaning. Don't disregard these interpretations. They are part of the personal messages that your guides are sending to you. Remember, your higher self is also your guide, and usually communicates through your sudden revelations and intuitive jumps.

What Does It Mean if I See Different Angel Numbers Within Minutes of Each Other?

This may happen after a meditation or when your angels and guides have a lot of different messages about various aspects of your life to convey. You might see a group of angel numbers that resonate most with your current career situation. Then, you might see a series of numbers that seem unrelated to the first ones, and these may refer to your love relationship or changes coming into your life.

Another reason may be because areas of your life are closely linked together. You know, like when you work with your twin flame or life partner, or your career advancement is dependent on your health. Or your new friend may inspire you down a different path in life or encourage you to travel. Then again, there's times when emotional weather is going to severely affect your work productivity over the next week.

Always remember: take what resonates and reassures. While angels and guides might warn you of difficulties, their ultimate intention is to reassure and support you through your manifesting and in difficult situations. Your intuition will let you know which of the angel number messages is yours.

Chapter 2:

Angel Numbers for Love

Love and romance is the one magical experience we all get to have, and the one that complicates our lives the most! There's always some little drama and trauma associated with it, if only internally, and this produces the most impact on our emotional and spiritual wellbeing. Naturally, when we're happy in love, our vibration and those around us are raised as well!

Angels and guides are our silent matchmakers, cheerleaders, and counselors in love and relationships. Just before you enter a significant relationship, during any hardships you may feel while in love, during any changes in love relationships, at the end of a relationship or a major life turning point for you and your partner, or when overcoming heartache, angel numbers will appear to guide you and support you through each phase. Your angels and guides may also be your love coaches, helping you heal and prepare for the most meaningful and love-filled relationships in your future.

If love, dating, and relationships are foremost in your mind, know that most angel numbers with strong love messages add up to or feature multiples of twos and the numeral six. Be careful not to squeeze all angel messages into your love inbox category. Often angels and guides will send an additional love sign—such as hearts or rings, or even ladybugs—to let you know the message is specifically related to your love situation.

Twos

Remember when at school how your friends used to transform 2 into a swan? Well, two has long been the symbol of romantic love and togetherness. It's no surprise, then, that the angels use it as the basis for many of their love messages.

2

When twos jump out at you, you're receiving continuous help from your angels, ancestors, and other benevolent guides to help you find or change your love situation in the way that you wish. "This is not a fluke. Follow your heart and instincts. Love is here!" is what they're saying to you. Whether it's finding your first love, a new love, or a renewal in love, what you see and feel is to be trusted. Rationalizing your feelings away will only work for a little while!

Twos can also communicate to singles that their single status is about change. A significant other will soon accompany you in the current activity or location you're in. Great news if you're walking by that romantic restaurant you'd love to dine in!

If you're at a distance from your love, your angels may send you a 2 to show that your loved one is thinking of you, too!

22

Spiritual love and your inner divinity is highlighted by this angel number. These two qualities are strong and important to your wellbeing and experience of love. Be patient in love, but ensure you're taking steps to meet love halfway as well. "Help us help you" is what your angels and guides are communicating. You may need to take some action, however little, to realize love. It may be time to start dating, change your dating sites, or take up a new hobby to meet new people. To refresh a love relationship, discuss what changes you'd like to see with your partner, then plan together. After all, your angels and guides can't do all the work for you!

Another message from 22 could be that while it may seem you and your love's paths are diverging, the resulting future events will draw you both together in a stronger bond or into a more stable situation. Sometimes, even true love needs some space to breathe and grow.

Similarly, 22 could also inform you that you and your love do have differences, but love wins through all!

222

This divine love number is sent to you by your Higher Self and angels to say that the path you're on is safe and right for you. Trust in the changes. They are leading to love. However, 222 could also be cautioning you: "Don't give so much of yourself in love that you lose yourself. Self-love is equally important as the love of another. It is safe for you to love, but love wisely!"

The number 222 could also signal that you have more options in love than you think. You have people around you with different but suitable traits: love and stability, love and passion, or a comfortable love that matches you in the way that seems easiest, and therefore rarest!

2222

With 2222, your angels and guides are trying their best to help you flag any issues around empowerment. They are saying, "It's up to you to advocate for yourself, even in your love and other relationships. Believe in yourself and your ability to have the future you dream of. Focus only on the important aspects of your life."

Twenty-two-twenty-two marks the coming of a period of peace and stability to your relationships. Together with your partner or future love partner, you'll experience material success. In other words, power couple vibes are all around you!

By placing twos throughout your space, your guides are confirming your decisions are well made and leading to greater progress in your life and love. Keep making those well-considered decisions!

3

With quirky threes bouncing around, your angels and guides send the message of encouragement and confirm that you're doing well in your inner work and outer world too! This is a number of romantic love, dating, and sometimes reunions. Your guides are expressing to you, "Pay attention to your intuition. It's leading you to a more cheerful and fun look at life and love. And this will bring in more love!" Often, threes means new beginnings: either a new love, or a reboot of an existing or old love.

Threes can also hint at an abundance of love around you. You may be adored or have secret admirers who may never come forward. That's not always a bad thing! Your guides and angels want you to know that you're very attractive and admired. This is amplified when you see sixes lingering around your threes or appearing soon after.

33

Do you feel love has passed you by or maybe you lack direction, not knowing how to find love at this time? Through 33, the angel message says, "Take heart! A new love is just around the corner. Divine protection and guidance is at play, so don't be afraid of opening your heart to love and life." It's a good time to remind yourself to stay heart-centered.

A current relationship may be renewed or become more romantic when your guides send you 33s. Great news if your partner has been distracted. It's likely that their angels are helping them set up a wonderful date!

When 33s just dot your landscape, love or a relationship is helping you fulfill an important spiritual contract in your life. Your relationship is aligned with your life purpose and will help you walk your path authentically. Consider yourself lucky to have a partner who understands your need to rush off to help those you feel called to aid or who gives you that special alone time to center and ground yourself each week.

6

If all you crave is a cuddle or a sweet kiss, you'll love the message of 6. "Physical love is close at hand or very significant now. Ensure you have a balance between the spiritual, the emotional, and the physical in this relationship," is what your angels are saying.

Sometimes, even though we wish for love and do our best to manifest it, we remain alone because our heart is fearful and closed to love. At times like these, your angels and guides will send you a 6 with the message in safe places and around trustworthy, kind people that it's safe for you to open your heart and allow this person into your heart. If there's no one significant about, then you may meet your next love, or divine life partner in or around the area you're in. All you have to do is allow yourself to love!

60

"Infinite, limitless love is around you. Unconditional love is here!" Sixty expresses your angels and guides' excitement for you. They invite you to celebrate the vibrations of love and expand them. It's time to share and be joyous with your loved ones. You don't have to miss out if you're single. Quite the opposite! Be good to yourself and take yourself out on a date. Live like your future partner is back home waiting for you and revel in the universal, limitless love swirling all around you.

64

There may be issues with control and dominance" is what your angels and guides wish you to know when you're dogged by 64s. Be mindful when dating a new person as they may be unhealthy control freaks in intimate relationships. If you're single, a block to love could be someone in your life controlling or dominating your life to the extent that it sabotages any new relationship. You'll need to draw boundaries with that family member or friend. If 64 is hanging about your current love relationship, you'll need to discuss boundaries with your love and ensure that neither of you feel unheard or disempowered by the other. Your angels and guides also want you to know that a playful competition between you and your spouse or new partner could be turning toxic. You needn't compete so hard or for their attention.

6666

You angels have much to say to you through 6666: "You embody love and compassion at this time, and are surrounded by the same. Be an example to others in showing and spreading compassion and love as you have a great influence on those in your environment. Be more open to those you love. Show more compassion to heal and change your relationship."

For singles and couples looking for a deeper love, 6666 is also a reminder that mature love is here or that your current relationship is maturing and evolving. For singles alone, your angels and guide have the advice that now is the time for you to define love anew.

808

Your angels confirm that you and your partner or future partner are equal in financial and other achievements. You suit each other perfectly. There'll be no secrets between you, and all matters will be handled with agreement and understanding. It's a wonderfully mature and eternal love! Neither of you will want for anything in this relationship!

Other Angel Numbers with Love Messages

1: When 1 carries a love message from your angels, they're letting you know that a new beginning in love is possible. And if you're an independent singleton, you'll remain so for a while longer. "Enjoy this special time by yourself. Do all the things you may not be able to do with your partner, or the partner you've envisioned," advise the angels. For a select few in coupledom, a solitary one may indicate that you may soon be single again. Look for nines that will confirm this. If no nines appear, you can safely disregard this particular interpretation.

333: With 333, your love message from the angels is, "Express yourself in this relationship. Reach out to someone." If you have a crush and the courage, it's okay to sound them out on whether your feelings may be reciprocated. Your angels also want you to know this: "Don't be afraid to be your true self. If your new love doesn't appreciate your authentic self, they may not be the one for you. You don't have to change yourself for love." Now, isn't that a relief!

555: Your angels need you to know it's time to let go of any energies from an old relationship or situation, as changes are bringing in a new cycle of love for you. This may also mean an old love is beginning a new chapter. For some, a relocation may be just around the corner and this means great things for your love life!

606: Your love match is out there! They are aligning with you. Both of you will have to go through a new beginning before you meet. For couples, both of you are mirroring each other in love. You get what you give!

626: Your angels bring you the assurance your future love is thinking of you, and that you're already connected in some way. When your frequency is high, you may dream of your future love and they of you. For couples in a long distance relationship, the same message applies, while for couples in close quarters, your angels want you to know that your partner is prioritizing you and your relationship as much as you are, even though they may remain quieter than a mouse!

726: "Open your eyes to love." Your angels and guides want you to know there's more to love than you currently perceive or there's someone close by who adores you. Another message of 726 is that you're viewing the person you're with, or the one you adore, with rose-colored glasses.

777: Things are getting more spiritual and mystical in love when your angels send you a 777 love message: "Great spiritual love, a very spiritual love, or a twin flame relationship is soon to begin." Expect to see even more synchronicities!

839: Whatever path you take is leading to growth and expansion. By harnessing your creativity and your generosity, you're attracting a greater and healthier love to you. Your current fears about love are ending and will be replaced by a lighter, more fun period in love and romance. Your current situation in love is teaching you a value balancing act that will enhance your love life very soon. Growing old together with your loved one won't ever get stale or boring as both of you inspire each other constantly and love each other's sense of humor!

888: There's various angel messages on love from 888. If you're tired of games and childish behavior, a new relationship is close at hand. It will mature quickly. And if you're a little oblivious, or don't believe you're attractive, your angels and guides are pointing out that a person who will be a good partner to you is in your vicinity. Everyone's favorite 888 message no matter their relationship status is: "The universe is helping you manifest the love and relationship you've always dreamed of!"

1010: The strongest message from 1010 is to trust your feelings and intuition about your love situation. Your angels and guides want you to remember you're more powerful in this relationship than you know. The second angel message from 1010 is that a spiritual love is coming your way, or a present love will now focus on your spiritual growth together. My favorite message from the angels is this: "The connection is perfect." Perfect!

1143 and 1144: Every relationship has some kind of secret, and some secrets you can't hide from! When 1143 or 1144 appear, your angels and guides are letting you know that, soon, secrets will be revealed and will result in a major change in your relationship. Not all secrets and changes are bad, so listen carefully and be sure to let your intuition and wisdom guide you.

1166: The message for 1166 can be a little complex, so bear with your angels and look for other signs to clarify its specific meaning to you. Spiritual love is growing between you and your loved one. Singles are likely to meet their next major person at a spiritual gathering. Together, your energies stimulate each other into a greater loving, wise, and spiritual whole. You could both conduct spiritual or philosophical meetings together and help fulfill each other's life path in a significant way. One partner is the leader and dominates the relationship. The other partner is the submissive and is happy to contribute whatever their partner requests from them. One partner has a wealth of ideas and is very masculine, the other partner may have great financial stability and resources and is quite feminine. Together, you complement and work well together. However, without the spiritual element, this relationship could easily fall into obsession and toxicity. Also, be wary of using and abusing the spiritual aspects and interests of this relationship. You may also want to look up 11 and 66 under [Twin Flames]().

1212: "Keep doing what you're doing in your quest for love as you're on your aligned path no matter how things seem." Your angels want you to know all is as it should be. There's no need to stress about your relationship or your single status. Things will work out as they should for everyone involved.

1234: With this progressive number, your angels are addressing your doubts about your relationships. Their message is: "Persevere. Your relationship still has some way to go together. Matters are improving quickly. If you are in an abusive relationship, you'll soon have help."

2121: With this number, your angels and guides have this happy message for you: "You and your partner or future partner make a great team without treading on each other's toes. There is no competition between you. There is nothing currently sabotaging your love and relationships." Sweet!

If you haven't found your angel number message here, Core Number Two sprouts more angel messages related to love and partnerships.

Chapter 3:

Angel Numbers and Messages for Twin Flames

With so many talking about their twin flames and twin flame journeys, it may be confusing if you aren't sure what these terms mean. I'd like to say it's simple, but it can get complicated because everyone's experience (and definitions, too) of a twin flame will vary. Luckily, everyone agrees that a twin flame is a higher-level (or very important) soulmate—the one who most forces you to evolve into a higher-level being. This often means they trigger you like no one else on earth! But it also means they'll teach you more about love and loving yourself than anyone else. Most twin flames usually have a spiritual and psychic connection as well as a special life purpose to realize together.

When someone speaks about their twin flame journey, they're talking about the time, the personal growth, and the future they hope to realize with their twin flame. Most twin flames and twin flame journeys are romantic and highly sexual in nature, but your dog or your cat can also be your twin, and so can a person you may only meet once for a few minutes. It's about the growth, the evolution, and the spiritual journey together.

Twin flame journeys can be scary as well as exciting and liberating. Besides your sudden spiritual growth, your guides and angels always try to prepare you for your next stage or to guide you through to the least painful route without avoiding those situations. There's also your twin flame and other people who are on your path towards greater expansion, enlightenment and your experience of unconditional, romantic ones throwing stuff at you all the time. Triggers and more triggers! Naturally, your guides and angels would like to pour some calm into the mix.

This means that you'll see a multitude of angel numbers just before and during your twin flame journey along with startling other synchronicities. You'll get indications your twin flame is about to cross your path, that it's time for reunion, and that it's time to step back or to move forward. Wherever you go in your twin flame journey, it's signposted by angel numbers to clue you in.

How often have you heard someone in the twin flame community enthuse every time they see eleven-eleven, or seven-eleven? While they may not necessarily be referring to the angel message, they see it as confirmation they're on their twin flame journey and in alignment with their twin. But looking deeper at the synchronicity and angel number meaning in context will add more to the messages the universe, the angels and your twin flame are sending you.

Keep in mind that if you're already on your twin flame journey, some messages may relate to other aspects of your life, too!

Ones and Elevens

1010

This can be referred to as ten-ten. Your angels and guides may often turn the clock, or turn *you* to the clock, to send this message about the heavier side of being a twin flame. "You and your twin are carrying heavy burdens, and these will soon be alleviated. Prepare for the next phase of your twin flame journey. You're about to exit your dark night of the soul phase and move onto a higher vibrational state." Great news if your dark night of the soul has been more than a drag!

11

This can be read as one-one or eleven. Depending on where you are on your twin flame journey, the message may differ. Listen to your intuition to filter through to the correct message for you. "There's more to life than this. Your twin may be thinking of you, but you may be on your own mission or vice-versa. A new personal cycle is beginning for you and your twin. Communication is key."

111

A key to manifesting is 111 with the angel message: "It's time for new beginnings and understanding of love and romance. Your manifesting abilities are very high at this time. Watch your thoughts and be aware of the kind of relationships you are currently creating." In other words, you may get *exactly* what you wish for, so dot your i's and cross those t's on your wishlist!

1101

You or your twin has dropped the ball. There's going to be a short break or difficulty in communication while the one fumbles through an unrelated situation. One of you is temporarily off your souls' path and will need some time and space before they can join the journey again.

1111

Often read as eleven-eleven. It's all about the journey with 1111. Your angels and guide use this message to often remind you of the basics of being on a twin flame journey because sometimes in the craziness we may tend to forget... "You are on your twin flame journey and are making progress. Be open to learning about unconditional love and redefining your concepts on love and self-love. You will experience telepathy. Remember, while you're in a twin flame relationship, you and your twin are equals and can either do the work together or as individuals. You are still in alignment with your path at this time."

1122

Your angels and guides want you to look and learn as being in a twin relationship is an education for your soul. "You will learn much from your twin flame at this time. They have mastered something you have not. Look, listen, and learn from them. If they're in proximity, you may observe some habit of theirs and unconsciously adopt it. This happens as part of your growth process." In other words, mirroring is fine and natural for twins as it's a way of gaining insights and wisdom quickly.

1212

There are a few messages with this one, depending where you are on your journey. Again, access your intuition to know which message speaks to you. "You and your twin are mirroring each other perfectly. This may be a way to confirm they're really your true flame and not a false flame." Does that address your doubts? I hope so!

"Your time has come to meet in 3-D. Expect to encounter them sooner than you thought. Your paths are perfectly aligned. Other aspects of your life are coming together to manifest your deepest, most cherished desires. Keep doing what you're doing." Wonderful news if you've been waiting for reunion since forever!

No contact? 1212 may signify your runner returning. Or that your chaser is back again. Your angels would like you to consider whether the runner-chaser dynamic is working for you. Is it time to address it further?

If you've completed this life's twin flame journey, the possibility of a new love is here if you choose to accept it. Remember, you're an empowered being of light and you chose your own experiences, even your twin flame ones.

2

A short and sweet message from your angels. "Reunion is close." Yay! This reunion can occur in person, on social media or other messaging, and also psychically in the fifth dimension. However you experience this reunion, you'll be able to enjoy a special togetherness.

22

Good news all around is announced by 22. The universe is helping you discover unconditional love, not just within your twin flame partnership, but with all beings! Your angels and guides also want you to know that you've passed a universal test with your twin flame and a positive change is coming your way.

222

Unconditional love and its challenges make up the theme for 222 messages. The angels and guides give reasons why you might be feeling so confused and angry, and how you might move forward in love. "You and your twin flame may not be in agreement. Differences between you are highlighted. Expect runner/chaser tendencies to resurface or be exaggerated. Can you find a way past this to the unconditional love you both embody and seek?"

For those newly on their twin flame journey, your angels and guides want you to know that what you're experiencing is real. If you aren't already aware of your divine mission on earth, you may soon be!

2121

When you spot 2121 often, your angels may be letting you know that the dynamics of your relationship with your twin is changing or has changed. The Runner may now be the Chaser. The one who had the lower vibration may now be the one with the higher vibration or seeing to spiritual matters.

Another message of 2121 is that you and your twin may take a few steps back. There may be no communication for a while as both of you pursue very different goals or regress into past behaviors.

2222

Yes, your 3-D and 5-D experiences with your twin flame are reciprocated and not just in your mind! Your angels may also want you to keep your senses primed as your twin is in your current 3-D environment. If you've not yet met them in 3-D, you're very likely to do so now.

2222 has a deeper meaning when it comes to vibrations. "Your vibration is higher than it's ever been and it's rising higher still. You are achieving part of your divine mission by maintaining and amplifying this loving, creative energy. For your twin and yourself, time and space are becoming meaningless." Wow! Just wow!

33

When 33s tumble through your days, issues around your twin flame journey are simplifying themselves. Greater clarity is here for you if you'll allow yourself to see it. Even under the magnifying glass, your love for your twin appears simple, elegant, and even innocent. Your angels and would like you and your twin to enjoy this playful, childlike, uncomplicated love.

33 may also bring the message that you may share ideas and like-minded solutions with your twin. Love and compassion surround you.

333

Three times three is at play with 333! You're dissolving karma and your spiritual growth is progressing well. Your work on yourself is also uplifting your twin and shortening your journey. Though this may be a difficult time, it will pass and you will reap benefits in more than just love.

333 may also signal that you may have to go over "old ground" more than once. Notice how you're shedding baggage. Notice how you're picking some up again. Rinse and repeat.

Your celestial team is helping you though you may not be aware of it and would appreciate it if you asked for help and guidance. They'll answer promptly. Remember, you are always supported and won't be asked to carry more than you can bear. The intensity of this energy may cause you and your twin to ghost each other.

444

When 444 is thrown at you, your personal foundations are solid and growing well. You shouldn't doubt yourself or what you've created. Though it may not appear so, your practicality is serving you and your twin very well.

444 also brings hope for those waiting on reunion: "The possibility of physical reunion remains strong, but you and your twin still have much work to do, either individually or together." Take heart. You're closer to reunion than ever before!

6999

You and your twin have completed and broken the karmic cycle between you or completed your souls' mission. You both have the choice to remain in this relationship or to move on. Pay close attention to other angel numbers and messages floating around to see what is the best path forward in love for each of you.

8

Infinity and passion are the hallmarks of this twin flame number. Your heavenly messengers want you to be aware of cycles, not just from your current life, but from your past lives, too. Break those cycles that no longer serve you.

8 is also referring to your passions. They run high, and your innate passion for a subject, person, or life is apparent to all. You may attract other suitors and your twin flame's or your fidelity may be tested in some way related to your current passion. It's a great time to set boundaries and expectations in your twin flame journey going forward.

88

88, reminiscent of the infinity sign twice over, brings a message about cycles. "You're in danger of repeating a cycle with your twin flame. This may be a negative or a positive cycle. Try to remain in your heart energy and ground yourself."

Other Angel Numbers for Twin Flames

10: The balancing of your inner masculine and feminine energies has begun. Don't be alarmed if you have a few mood swings. You'll soon feel yourself, only with more clarity.

17: Your angelic team is marking the start of your twin flame journey! "The beginning of your twin flame journey is imminent. Time to research twin flames or search deeper into the theories and experiences to prepare for your own journey. Avoid falling into the belief that your life needs to revolve around reunion with your twin. It revolves around your evolution, otherwise known as ascension."

66: Your twin is inspiring you or acting as your muse in life. You may explore expressing yourself differently, particularly in a creative way. You may change or spend more time on your appearance. Remember you are your own person and it's not healthy to compromise all that you are for your twin's desires and wishes. Yours matter, too! You may also want to read 66.

69: You may experience unconditional love for the first time, and this may be self-love. 69 tells you you're strong enough to move on from situations and find greater love and happiness. Matters may flip constantly and unpredictably. Some of this may be due to astrological events such as Mercury Retrograde or Venus and Mars retrogrades. Stay grounded in your heart. You and your twin may be flipping between your masculine and feminine energies erratically.

234: Progression and teamwork are highlighted. You're making headway on your twin flame journey. Together with your twin, you may be doing 5-D and higher work together that supports your joint lives' mission at this time. You could be sending love and light together to parts of the earth and a collective that greatly needs it. You may both be inspired jointly or individually to change your direction in life or your careers in order to realize an idea that can uplift the planet!

414: You and your twin are mirroring your drive and need for stability. This may mean you may have to walk alone for some time. Your guides and angels always surround you and are helping you find or maintain some kind of stability. This may mean the ending of a few long-term connections in your life, temporary and permanent.

555: There's a lot going on with a 555 message. "A series of triggers will bring Tower moments and a possible shadow and transformation period. It's time to address your shadow issues and those of your twin flame, too. If you're feeling overwhelmed and that the world doesn't understand you or that everything's a challenge, you may be in the dark night of the soul phase. Seek support from friends and family. It will pass as soon as you've integrated your lessons." Remember, what's cleared away makes room for something better to come in!

666: There's some straight-talk from your celestial team. "You need to raise your vibration or protect your energy. This isn't a negative number or message, but issues of addiction (hard and soft), ego-driven decisions, feelings of entitlement, and unhealthy bondage to ideas, work, or people are keeping your vibrations on the lower scale. Be careful of obsessing over your twin flame, especially sexually, and their current life. Remember, this is your journey, and theirs may be quite different."

711: It's about you and your fortitude. "For this stage of your journey you walk by yourself and you have the support and love of your guides and your twin."

717: You are protected—even from yourself! Inexplicable events may delay or cancel plans that might have led to much hardship and pain. Your guides want you to reconnect with your intuition. Approach any situation with love. Being alone may be physically frustrating, but know that this, too, is part of your growth and work. Avoid jealousy over others in your twin's current circle.

777: Yay! Luck is changing for the better. Your manifesting of material and financial help or independence is a success. 777 confirms your abundance is growing, as is your twin's. Your spiritual practices and connections are very strong at this time. The universe is applauding you for the work you've already done, and the work you still have to do.

911: Well done! "You've mastered one phase of your evolution and are about to begin the next chapter at a higher frequency. You may experience other dimensions or find that you feel more confident of yourself and your choices this far. You and your twin may be slightly out of step with one of you at a higher vibration. The other twin will have to master some aspect of themselves to match the other."

Chapter 4:

Angel Numbers for Grief and Lost Loved Ones

During times of grief, we isolate ourselves or feel that no one can understand the pain we feel at the time. The angels and your guides do. They stand beside you as you cry and do your best to honor who or what has passed away. Then, they gently show you the easiest way forward to rejoin the world of the living. Occasionally, they may send you messages about your lost loved ones.

Angel Numbers for Those in Grief

44

The appearance of this number may be a message from your angels or a deceased loved one. Both your deceased loved ones and your angels would like you to heal, move forward in life, and find happiness again. Be happy with where you are today. Show gratitude for all the good in your life. They challenge you to write a gratitude list with 44 items on it! These can be things and people from your past or present, but ensure it's a true and balanced list.

222

"It's time to make a decision," says your angelic team. Whatever you decide will be fine, but you *must* make a decision. They cannot help you further until they know which direction you choose to go. If you don't make a decision, you risk being disempowered when others make decisions that are yours to make. Do it for your future and those that depend on you. Go on. Make that decision.

333

333 reminds you to take a look around. "You have support and love all around you. Don't disregard what is in front of you. Be grateful for those who support you and wish to see you happy again. Allow them closer to your heart."

555

Change is here, no matter how you feel about it. You, too, must change. Don't worry. The changes will be easier than expected and once you're accustomed to it, you will appreciate all the goodness they bring to your life. Through every change, your angels and guardians will surround you.

666

You are stronger than you think. You can get through this. There is light at the end of the tunnel and that light is you! Your angels and guides want you to know that they will help you find the light within yourself again; that spark of confidence; that belief that life holds good ultimately for us all.

777

You may be missing something, because your angels are saying, "The miracle you're searching for is happening though it may not look like or take the course you want. Open up your mind and heart and see with clarity what is truly happening. Then you'll see the true miracle."

888

888 is sent by your celestial team to help you release. The material doesn't matter anymore. It's okay to release, let go of things of only material worth, and clear the energies around you. What matters most is your personal strength, your self-worth, and your spiritual growth. If you've lost a loved one, realize that their material body was not the sum of them. Neither were their possessions. Celebrate their smile, their jokes, their cooking; and do the same for you. You will find replacements or no longer need material things to maintain your loving memories and spiritual connection. Nor do you need stimulants to find your creativity. Allow the healing to begin.

999

The worst is over. The only steps to take are the ones that move forward. You'll begin to feel acceptance of the situation and see changes for the better. Your usual sense of energy and purpose will return soon. You'll feel more comfortable with others around you once more. You've been so strong, and so good. The angels thank you and will remain beside you for as long as you need them.

1221

Your angels and loved ones in spirit are urging you to resume your normal routine. "The foundation to your career and other relationships is solid. It's not worth risking all you've built at this time. It's also time to take better care of yourself. You have the support you need. If you find you can't cope while back at work or during your daily routine, it may be time to call a therapist or other healer. Grieving so intensely over such a long period is hurting you and those that count on you. You can and will piece yourself and your world back together." 1221 is their hug to you.

Angel Numbers for Lost Loved Ones

222

Your lost loved one is helping you find love! This may be a person, a pet, or even a new hobby. It hurts them to see you still pining for them. They want you to experience all that love can offer.

333

When you spot 333 often after losing a loved one, they and your angels want you to accept that this chapter of your life is closed. Living your life for the one you've lost isn't healthy for you. Accept the ending. Recognize that others need you at this time. Be there for the others who were also left behind.

444

Your loved one wants you to know that they are fine. There's no need to worry about them. All is well between you. They would also like to remind you of something fun or creative you'd promised to do but haven't. They advise you on following that whim now! Go to that art class. Go on that vacation. Go visit your best friend from across the country. There's something they want you to see or experience while doing so.

888

Their love for you transcends time and space. If you believe in reincarnation, you'll meet again. If you don't, they will continue to carry their love for you through their next phase of being. They appreciate your time together, and your love, but they must now journey without you, as you must without them.

922

Your loved one is further transitioning into their next phase of being. They may not be reachable at times, or they are turning into a spirit for you. Don't be sad. It's a very exciting time for them, and if they've been deemed worthy to be your guide in spirit, they are very much honored and well regarded in the spirit realm. Be happy for them. And allow any grief or sorrow you feel to dissolve. In the days to come, you'll think of them less and less as you begin to reclaim much of the energy you spent grieving. Or if they are your spirit guide, your relationship will change slightly. This doesn't mean the love isn't there, just that you're both getting to where you need to be next. Watch for the signs, dreams, random songs, and (of course) angel numbers they'll send you to communicate more easily with you.

1212

Your lost one is working to introduce you to a wonderful new acquaintance or friend. You will share and understand each other's experiences and comfort each other. You won't feel lonely or alone again! This new person will introduce you to a healing modality or help you understand your grief and loved ones better.

Chapter 5:

Angel Numbers About Change

Changes in life can be scary, especially if you have to go through them alone, among people who make you feel inferior and who don't (or choose not to) understand you. Not much may be unchanging at such times, except for your celestial cheerleaders and supporters! Whether you're going through a relocation, a new job, a medical or phase-of-live change, your angels and guides will cheer your progress, aid where requested, and ensure you receive support or intervention should they be needed. Pay close attention. Your celestial guides don't wish to see you apprehensive about any changes.

How Angels Signal a Change Coming Into Your Life

Angels and guides may send you various angel numbers as they do for other aspects of your life. However, when a huge change is headed your way, or they wish you to begin preparing for your future (sometimes this may be over several years), your heavenly messengers tend to send you a series of progressive sequences. For example, if you have to prepare for a massive change such as a relocation or emigration, you might begin by seeing 09:09, then 00:00 followed by 10:10. Next, you might see 14:14, 15:15, and 16:16, and end the day with 19:19. Your guides are encouraging you to organize and gather the skills, the documents, the funds, and anything else you require because this new beginning may arrive either unexpectedly, or at what may look like an inopportune moment. Most times, we say that this change begins with divine timing!

Don't forget that other angel messages and signs will be sent to you, too. Continuing the example of relocation, you might see a phone number with the digits 00 over the country or state you feel drawn to consider. At home, you may get calls or messages at 9:00 or 09:09, signaling your home will soon change. Around the same time, you may see 555 at unexpected moments underlining a skill you may need to develop.

By paying attention to these messages of preparing for change, our guides lead us through intimidating transitions with ease—life's transitions the stress-lite way!

00

Heads-up! An important new beginning is arriving fast! This may mean something else is ending. It could be that a new job means the loss of a good friendship, or you may be located further away from your favorite coffee shop. Your angelic messengers are communicating, "Don't fear for what you're leaving behind. Something equally good or better will replace it once the new beginning arrives."

1

The first step in a new beginning is arriving or is already here. Your guides elaborate with, "Don't be afraid to move into this new situation. You have the skill, the knowledge, and the energy to succeed. All you need to add is confidence. Being bold now will set a good tone for the near and mid-term future."

"This new beginning is bringing you greater independence as well as alignment to your top priorities. There's unity and strength available for you to lean on should you feel you need it." Angels are all around you, even earthly ones!

With one as your angel number, another message on a new beginning says that the change may raise your status and reputation. "You may find yourself in a position of greater authority than you're comfortable with. Accept that others may perceive greater things in you than you do yourself. Don't fight this change. Be who you need to be."

3

Through threes, your heavenly guides are signaling that they are working on illuminating your path forward. Through your intuition, the play of light on objects, numbers, words, and people, they are guiding you toward helpers who will make any transitions an easy one for you.

The changes that three brings include greater abundance: having more people around you, more material things, more time, or more money. Your guides add, "Another person may have a say in this change or the situation that follows, so this change may not be entirely in your control. It's for you to allow the flow of abundance and enjoy it at this time regardless." Continue regardless!

5

With five popping up to announce a change, it may be quite an exciting one! The angels are telling you not to worry as that only creates blockages that may slow down the transitions and transmutations or make them appear more difficult. Accept the changes. You'll surprise yourself at how quickly you'll adapt to the new!

With a multitude of fives around, times may be a little unpredictable. The angels request you don't make long-term plans, but instead, remain flexible. Travel may be difficult at this time, so when it comes to tickets and accommodation, you may want to ensure there are no hidden penalties for sudden cancellations.

Depending on the area you live in, and if all is well and stable in your life, unexpected appearances of five, or a string of them in strange positions or off-kilter, may be a sign from your celestial team that severe weather is on the way: tornados, hurricanes, high winds, blizzards—any severe weather that may require you to pick up a little more food or water at the store and ensure all batteries are accessible and charged. You may also want to ensure the dog or cat have their beds in a safe area indoors.

9

When you see nine repeatedly in context to a person's body, your angels and guides may be conveying that your body is undergoing changes. A chapter of your life may be closing. They would like you to do your annual health checkup if you haven't already, or make that appointment you've been putting off all this time. While they don't want to alarm you, there is something related to your body that you need to attend to or understand at this time.

By sending you nines, your angels and guides could also be celebrating the fact that your financial situation may be improving! You may be on the final installment of a large debt, or you could be getting an unexpected raise or promotion. It may not be much, but each month you'll have a little more cash in your wallet for some little well-deserved luxuries.

Another message from nines accompanying you through your day is that you're finally getting some time to yourself. You may be on your own for a while: a few hours to a few days. You'll have time to meditate, reflect, and prepare yourself for the next phase in your life or year. Sometimes, nines can also be a message about isolation. You may have made a weekend booking with friends, but find you have to drive yourself or use the accommodation alone. Most of the time, this may come as a relief to you, but sometimes, it can be a gentle reminder to ensure you have something to while away your time and not depend on others to carry anything essential that you may be needing.

Your friends 'upstairs' may send you nines when you doubt yourself during a process of change, particularly in your "What am I doing here?" moments. Spotting a nine is the universe sending you a confirmation that you're currently on your life path, even if the circumstances seem unlikely or unrelated. Trust in the process.

22

Twenty-two or two-two carries the message that the changes you're experiencing bring greater stability to your life. What you build now in love, relationships, home, and your career will remain in your life for a long while or until the next major chapter on your life path is completed.

The twin twos could also be a message that the change brings collaboration and teamwork that will half your burden in some way. Yay!

With 22 appearing often, your heavenly guides are hard work informing you that you're coming to a crossroads in your life, career, love life, or other major issue. The angels are saying, "The paths offered to you may mirror each other and will ultimately draw you to the same destination. This is especially applicable to those who feel themselves drifting away from family and friends."

For more information about possible changes coming your way via 22, read 22 The Master Builder.

123

When it comes to changes, seeing 123 is a wonderful sign that things are happening as they should. Your guides may be quite stern about this time period. "There are no short-cuts. Levels will be reached and completed before the next level can be attained."

Occasionally, your angels and guides may be advising you to take a step back if you feel uncomfortable in a situation, particularly if that process or change was already mapped out to you. You may need a little more research or someone's professional (or local) help at this time. Ensure you haven't missed any steps or important paperwork at this time.

123 is also a playful sign from your celestial team that is meant to assure you that the process of change is simpler than you imagine. "Matters will proceed smoothly and in a logical fashion. You won't be caught off-step." And don't overthink things!

Another message that 123 carries is, "At this time, the changes are predictable, or have been predicted to you or by you!"

555

This angel number is preparing you for a significant change in your life. Though you may not be aware of what this change might be, your guardian angels don't want you to be caught off-guard or to hesitate when this amazing change occurs. This transition could be a series of small changes that add up to a significant life change, or a major one that shifts your life into a new direction. You may begin seeing this number quite a while before any perceived changes occur as it's a message and reminder to continue preparing.

919

919 brings a short, reassuring message. "A temporary, but necessary, change is here."

This angel number is another used as confirmation by your guides that a chapter in your life is over and that it's time for the new one to begin.

1010

1010 is a message about evolution: "You have evolved out of your current situation, particularly when it comes to your work and income. This time is favorable to seek situations and clients. Be bold, be confident." New changes at this time suit you and most will be impressed by you. Keep that confidence going!

1010 is also sent by your angel team when it comes time to notify you about growing your success. You may receive a series of small tasks or commissions that build your confidence and skills very quickly. You'll impress with your ability to meet deadlines and delivery as expected and this will lead to bigger and better outcomes in your new future.

Other Angel Numbers Indicating Coming Changes

511: A big transition may seem riskier than it is as it's asking you to change at a deeper level than you'd like. The inner work you do for this transformation is leading to a greater spiritual expansion and a new, more successful phase of your life. Be adventurous. See where life is leading you!

911: One situation ends while another, much more significant situation is about to begin when you spy 911 at each turn. You have the opportunity now to build stronger, better, more lasting relationships, careers, homes, and new projects. What you envision at this time may have a strong positive impact on the world around you.

At its core, number 5 brings change, while core number 9 brings endings. The appearance of either of these digits could indicate the angel number message relates to change. For more messages on changes, look at Core Number Five and Core Number Nine.

Chapter 6:

Angel Numbers Regarding Friends and Friendships

As with most facets of our lives that impact our wellbeing, your heavenly guides take great interest in your friends. They'll send messages about new friends arriving, old friends reappearing, troubled friendships, and trustworthy friendships. In this way, your celestial team helps you weed out frenemies, too—but only once you've gotten your lesson from that relationship!

Why Angels Send You Messages About Friends and Friendships

We tend to forget the importance of our friendships and acquaintances. After our romantic relationships, depending on family ties, friendships have the most impact on our daily lives, and happiness, too! A souring of a long friendship or a broken friendship can cause as much pain as a romantic break-up. We place such great trust in our friends that what they say and how they react to us changes how we feel about ourselves and our creations. Often, the criticism of a friend from school can stick with us for much of our adulthood.

Think about all the times good friends, and friends with similar interests (even if temporary), gave you the companionship and motivation to expand your world. Their enthusiasm may still introduce your next love, next hobby, or next job. Friends 'get' your passion for your newest craze or lifelong interest. They commiserate over bad dates, lost opportunities, and challenging bosses. Much like your angels, your healthiest friendships give you someone who's got your back in an often bewildering and unpredictable world.

While your celestial guides may send a message to your friend to give you a call on a bad day, your friend's sympathy is what makes you feel better after that frank chat and a cup of coffee. Naturally, your guides and angels will look out for both of you by sharing messages between you.

111

111 brings the following message about friendships: Intense and significant relationships and connections may form at this time, challenging and changing your beliefs and routines. This is temporary. Most of these new friends or frenemies are likely to leave your life soon and unexpectedly. They come into your life to teach you about yourself and to help you expand. Some may be soul mates, others not. Of the one or two who stay longer in your life, they may travel the same path as you for longer, but they, too, may leave when your paths diverge.

Some of these friends and friendships may be cyclic, coming around as you begin new spiritual chapters in your life, then parting as you get deeper into your personal life paths. The angels may call these friends your spiritual classmates!

211

You may join a circle of friends who've been together for quite some time, possibly since childhood. At times, the group dynamics may be overwhelming or cause restrictions in your life. Your celestial team sends the message that you grow stronger from the experience. Your guides also remind you to stay true to yourself and to your beliefs no matter how seductive their lifestyles may be. These friends are here to show you who you truly are.

Sometimes, 211 may indicate couple friendships or family friendships that teach you much about yourself or that may help you with your career.

212

212 presence announces a new significant friend is entering your life. You may not immediately click or even get along, but once you get to know each other a little better, you'll find that you share the same adventurous or stay-at-home spirit. This new friend may be your new partner-in-crime when it comes to having the kind of fun you both enjoy. Together you may encourage each other to perfect certain skills or share experiences others in your life may not care for. This person may be your weekly lunch date, your book-club buddy, or even the person you exchange and practice your tarot readings with.

414

A new friend may enter your life at the beginning of a transition in your life or theirs. While you may only know each other briefly or remain in the same place for a little while, they will help you find success and spiritual growth, and you will reciprocate. This is the friend who may move across town or across the country, but still raves about you to their new friends, sending goodwill, support, and lots of opportunities to grow your career or your business. They'll like your social media and chat often with you. When you meet again, you'll pick up where you left off. The angels want you to know that this friend is a rock you can count on even if they aren't physically beside you.

616

With 616 appearing often, themes and issues of generosity and compassion in your friendships are being underlined. The angels want you to know that it's okay to break off friendships where your generosity and compassion are constantly abused.

If you're constantly throwing pity-parties or taking certain friends for granted, your angels gently remind you with 616 that you are not being fair to your friends. You can do much to be a better friend. Alternatively, if you're smothering your friends, 616 comes along to remind you that everyone needs some space, and sometimes too much generosity is too much of a good thing for some personalities. Keep your friendships healthy and content.

If your friendships are equal and reciprocal, you may see 616 when a friend is going to introduce you to your next love. For some, a platonic friendship may also shift into a love relationship. Your angels and guides are letting you know it's time to say yes to blind dates arranged by friends you trust or to give your friend a chance at love. They just might be the One you've been looking for!

777

You're blessed with a wonderful friendship. There's a lot of synchronicities and magic around when you're together. You may get complimentary gifts or products when out shopping together or dining out. You might find time aligns perfectly on the days that you meet or hang out together. Unplanned surprises bring joy and fun. Your friend may share your spiritual beliefs or practices, and you'll have deep conversations that may go on for hours.

Sometimes 777 shows a mentor coming in as a friend, or a mentor becoming a personal friend. Both of you will learn a lot from each other.

Other Angel Numbers With Friendship Messages

811: Friendship blessings come to you from a new friend or a friend you can always count on. This may be regarding a new venture or other big change in your life.

818: You're about to meet a soulmate friend, one who may have shared lifetimes with you. Your angels confirm that their familiarity at first sight is because you *are* soul mates. This will be an instant friendship that lasts for as long as you have the same path to walk in this lifetime.

1155: A friend may challenge you and help your self-growth. Your guides send the message that you'll work well with this friend on practical matters or business as one of you takes the initiative while the other has a wealth of ideas. Both of you are aligned to the same goals.

1212: A friend may introduce you to someone who will take center stage in your life. This will be a blessed relationship with an abundance of laughter, creativity, and positive energy.

2353: You and your friend are feeding each other's self-doubts. It's time for you both to be bold and allow your natural talents to blossom. Help each other find more positive ways and words to communicate and change each other's vibrations. You could speak affirmations together and hold each other accountable when developing healthier and more positive vibrations.

Chapter 7:

Angel Numbers With Recurring Ones

Number one speaks of innovation, individuality, and the individual. It's also considered a number for personal strength because it stands tall alone, not depending or leaning on any other number. Most of all, ones refer to new beginnings in all aspects of your life. One is also universally regarded as the number of a leader.

When you see sequences of ones, the major meaning of the digit in your current context is amplified and modifies other numbers grouped with it.

Core Number One

This number highlights your personal power. If it's sent to you often, it may be that your career and finances are rebooting or that you're in a good phase to make accelerated progress in those areas. You may be offered a new job or be given a promotion. You may be given a new financial opportunity. Seeing one often is sure encouragement that you can be bold and safely express your individuality or try new things.

One is a shout-out to you that your ideas and future plans are safe and healthy for you to follow. Let the courage of one sweep you into setting foot on that journey you've always delayed or thought you'd never have the courage to take, for one resonates with your pioneering and reliant spirit.

One is also gently reminding you that you are setting an example to those around you or who are in your circle. Some may prefer you to lead in a community or collaborative setting.

When signaling new directions, one may refer to a new burst of creativity and optimism. This message is often seen by those in the creative field or who are in danger of becoming stuck in a pessimistic frame of mind.

Remember that one is singular. You may be entering a time when you may work better alone or prefer to work or be in isolation. The appearance of one is also a cheer from the angels and guides when you've taken the steps to celebrate and share your originality and enthusiasm for matters that are aligned with your life path and for the highest good of all; even if it is only in sharing a doodle or creating an inspired meme. You are being encouraged to continue helping to raise the vibration of those that you interact with.

The appearance of one can also seek to prepare you for a challenge ahead. It may be that your voice is the only one that is raising concern over an obvious safety hazard or injustice. You may also face isolation and discrimination because you are perceived as different or not toeing the line. Or, your authority may be challenged. One is urging you to respond with the compassion you'd wish to receive. One strengthens and shows a better way forward for all.

Most would be happy to know that one signifies success! Whether in your career, artistic pursuits, love, or other challenges, having ones appear out of the blue is a sure sign you are in the process of achieving success if you've not already attained it.

11

The first of three master numbers in numerology, 11 or eleven brings the message that your psychic ability is being awakened or it's growing in leaps and bounds. At this time you may experience prophetic dreams, amazing synchronicities and meet remarkable teachers and people on a similar path as you.

With eleven, angels and guides remind you that your inspiration may strike continuously and at the most unexpected moments. It's a wonderful time to keep notes for future creative projects.

Your imagination may be boundless, and if you cannot sustain a high enough vibration, you may suffer bouts of anxiety. Whenever you feel overwhelmed, you may ask your angels and guides to feed you any new ideas, downloads, and gifts when you feel better able to cope or in a slower manner so you can assimilate and receive them without overwhelm. Your angels and guides always listen to your needs first.

Elevens, along with ones, are the numbers of the inventor and of ingenuity. Seeing elevens, even in your dreams and daydreams, encourage you to follow your ideas through as you're in a period of ingenious problem-solving.

When this master number shows up erratically, you may feel compelled to explore universal and cosmic truths. Your angels and guides are reminding you that they will follow and protect you whenever and wherever you call on them.

111

For freelancers and those who manage clients, 111 can indicate new projects or clients who will make your reputation or bring you some prestige. Your angels and guides are supporting you through this time by cheering you on and sending you inspiration and belief in your ideas and style.

You may straddle the world of spirituality, different collectives and circles, as well as of your career and responsibilities with ease. Your spiritual insights might resolve conflicts with difficult people or situations at work or at home, and you may interact with vastly different people with understanding and mutual respect—even affection.

There may be a clash of personalities around you. Your guides want you to know that all concerned have valid points and that balance and agreeing to disagree, yet still working to the same goal would be best for all.

111 could also be sent to you when there is a major reset in your life. You may have to leave frivolities or maintain a minimalist approach for the time being. Simplify, then simplify again. What you choose to discard now will greatly affect the ease of your journey ahead. The more you remain open to future growth instead of current materialism, the faster your progress will be. Choose wisely what you hold close. A series of new beginnings will pare down your decisions until there is only the most illuminated path for you.

1111

Your spiritual growth is accelerated. With the doubling of the first Master Number, your spiritual growth positively affects all other areas of your life. You may be actively manifesting or merging your current interests, skills, and your divine life path at this time. The angels and guides cheer your success!

Your successes are also doubled or quadrupled at this time. Don't be surprised if you're flooded with requests for your product, services or insight. Opportunities seem boundless and you may choose any safely. New beginnings in one sphere of your life now, lead to new and better beginnings in other spheres of your life soon.

Chapter 8:

Angel Numbers With Recurring Twos

Number two is that of togetherness and duality. It is also the number that relates to balance, justice, and negotiation to facilitate those. Two reminds one of partnerships and commitments, bonds and promises. For most of us, two is the number of romantic love and all that is needed to make relationships succeed.

Sequences of twos such as 222, 2222, and 22:22 amplify the essential meaning of the digit. In sequences such as 12:12 and 123, it also modifies the numbers next to it.

Core Number Two

It's hard to find a greater indicator that partnerships are being highlighted. Two appears when you may be feeling isolated and alone to remind you that even if you may be physically alone, you still have your angels and guides around you, working with you. For a few, particularly light-workers, this angel number may reveal that your guides, ancestors, and angels wish to work more closely with you, or that a new guide will soon be highlighting your next steps on your soul's journey.

Two urges you to seek balance or to redress sudden imbalances. In matters of finance and money, it may point to your bank balance and ask you to consider if your spending versus earning tendencies are healthy for you. In business partnerships, it could point to an uneven distribution of responsibilities.

Two may signify to singles and those looking for serious relationships that a high-level soulmate like a twin flame or divine life partner is on their way to you. It promises that you won't be feeling single for very much longer.

For those already in love and engaged, two often foretells your dreams of marriage or a wedding are close at hand. Beware, the angels do have a sense of humor, and if your yearning is greatest for buying that wedding dress or wedding cake, you may do so, but it could all be for your favorite cousin or friend!

If you've asked for guidance on how to move forward in a situation, two is sent by your angels to advise cooperation. They also assure you that being flexible and adaptable at this stage will bring the highest potential outcome to you. Working alone or aiming for extreme independence could sabotage your efforts and any projects at this time. Teamwork is the key to success in any of your relationships for now. Set aside differences and work to each other's strengths. Pulling together now makes the whole much stronger and long-term prospects more viable.

If you're being ambushed by twos, the angels are underlining that negotiation is required. Are you being too stubborn in a situation? Are you accepting matters unquestioningly? Is your new contract really as fair to you as previously or do you need to renegotiate your salary, your hours, or your responsibilities? As long as fairness and balance are sought with mutual respect, negotiations needn't mean heavy compromise, but rather cooperation and a win-win situation for all.

The appearance of two could also be a reminder that you may need to place yourself in someone else's shoes to gain a greater understanding of the person, community, or situation. Greater empathy will help heal the situation at this time.

Another less common meaning of two is that there could be two issues at play or that need to be addressed simultaneously. Don't be alarmed if you feel this meaning resonates with you. Your angels and guides won't leave you overwhelmed.

22

The second of the master numbers in numerology, 22 is often called the Master Builder. With its appearance, your guides are bringing into your awareness the greatest of your potentials and that this is the right time to begin realizing it.

Twenty-two may indicate remarkable success in material and practical matters as well as in spiritual matters. The angels want you to keep in mind that what you build now will have far-reaching consequences, so build well and use this blessed time responsibility.

This master builder message merges dualities: thought and feeling, feminine and masculine, old and new, intuition and fact. While this merging may sound and look chaotic at times, your guides and angels are assuring you that the outcomes will be an enduring and sustainable better reality. You may also experience shifts in timelines and realities.

Ground and envision, vision-board, and visualize only what you wish to see and experience in your future.

At this time, major shifts in the collective will favor your future vision. Around you and even worldwide, changes in policies, planning, structure, and trends will align with you or you with them. Your circle, or society at large, may also change or accept mergers or mergings that might have been frowned upon before. This may include marriage and other relationship and friendship aspects.

By bringing you Master Builder 22, your angels and guides are showing their belief in you and your ability to create and co-create with the world around you in a sustainable, beautiful, and honorable way.

222

This number brings assurance. Your spiritual team is around you 24-7 during any difficulties. No matter what is going on in your family, love, or work situation, your angels and guides are there to support and help you.

Your angels and guides remind you that with positive thoughts and love you can achieve anything even without the expected or yearned-for support from those in your circle. Ask yourself what is possible at this time, then disregard it because everything is! Follow your dreams!

Let your intuition fill in the blanks. Events will move into a positive and healthy phase once you do.

2222

You'll meet your match soon! Your angels and guides send you this message so you can recognize your match in love, teamwork, business partnership, or even opposition. You'll recognize this person by their being or sounding very much like you! Even if you are in opposition, there'll be respect and even an exchange of mutual regard and ideas to everyone's satisfaction. Ultimately, their goals may be the same as yours, but their methods and approach may differ.

Twenty-two-twenty-two brings a great lesson with an even greater reward. If you can resolve and integrate this lesson's core, you will benefit from it for the rest of your life. In many cases, those around you will benefit too, particularly if a situation has to do with the world at large.

The angels and guides are cheering at your finding a balance that is sustainable and stable. This balance will provide a firm base for you to grow into limitlessness and integration of all your energies. It's a wonderful confirmation that part of your ascension journey has been achieved and recognized.

Chapter 9:

Angel Numbers With Recurring Threes

If the number three were to be personified, it would be the ever cheerful, superbly creative, bursting with optimism person getting all the shy ones at the dance to join in the fun while being totally unselfconscious about their own charisma and magnetism.

Core Number Three

Like all good things, three has its challenging side, too. Three can harbor or generate conflict, especially interpersonal conflict, without meaning to. It can offer you one choice too many, or indicate that someone—most likely you—may be feeling like a third wheel. When you see threes recurring, your angels and guides are reminding you to think a little deeper about the consequences; about how your words and actions may be misinterpreted and to attempt crystal-clear communication where possible; about your contributions or presence in the situation; and about the long-term effects your choices might hold. Indeed, the long-term effects may ultimately determine your best choice. Even with these reminders, the angels don't wish to inhibit you, only to guide you in a way that minimizes misunderstandings and missteps.

Threes announce your creativity and problem-solving abilities are outstanding and will reward you. People find you engaging and charming. They are ready to pay attention to you, your messages, and your creations. In some way, the spotlight might fall on you. Sometimes, if you work mainly from home, the angels may be hinting it's time to pay a little more attention to your appearance before you step out in case you end up on camera or run into someone who will expand your network and reach greatly!

Threes highlight that the idea or project you're currently thinking about is the one to run with! Collaborations with more than one person may also go well.

For some who wish to have a child, angels will send the number three to confirm that your little one is on the way. This may be true for those seeking furbabies, too.

If you're confused over work or love, your guides may announce that you've reached a fork in the road with three options and that it's time to actively exercise your free will by making a conscious decision by choosing one path. This doesn't mean that the other two paths are lost to you forever, only that you can only focus your energies on one at this particular time.

Recurring threes also announce a joyful time is here, as is generosity. The three-fold rule may be at play when you share the joy and extend your generosity to others so share the fun, the joy, the good fortune, and the love as much as you wish!

With threes, angels and guides are whispering that it's time to write that book, to draw and paint that scene, to make that jewelry, or start the DIY project whether it's fixing the bookshelf or remodeling the house. Every creative pursuit will bring you joy and satisfaction in the long term because three is the number of creation. It's your time to create!

33

Master number 33 is the rarest number in numerology. To have your angels and guides send you 33s is a sign that they are throwing graduation hats at you! Though this graduation may refer to your spiritual attainment, it could also be in academics, for 33 identifies the Master Teacher. If school and class strike you cold, don't worry. Others may seek you as a mentor or guru at this time, or simply value you for your insight and calm, compassionate vibe. The message your guides are sending you is to be generous, but not smothering with your compassion, care, and insight. Your guides may also be whispering that you should only offer advice at this time if it's requested.

By sending you 33s, other masters may enter your life or offer you guidance from the spiritual realm. Meditations will be deep and profound. These masters will be approachable and, in most cases, generous with their knowledge.

With 33 being the combination of the previous master numbers, all their high frequencies plus more are now available to you. Your dreams may once again be prophetic, but with your creativity and ingenuity, you may find that some outcomes may be avoided—if they are aligned with your path.

By sending you 33s, your guides and angels are acknowledging your giving nature and tendencies which may be very great at this time.

Even if those around you don't notice your generosity and benevolence, the universe is noting it.

With 33s around, healing is also occurring and kundalini awakenings may be happening to you. Your focus will be humanitarian and global. Your angels and guides will help you find others who share the same motivation of altruism to benefit future generations and current beings in distress. Lucid dreaming and visualizing at this time will be easier, helping you self-heal faster.

If you're feeling depleted by constantly attending and serving those around you, 33 is a message that it's time to show yourself the same care and nurturing. No one expects you to solve everyone's problems 24-7!

333

You may have some unusual and ascended guides around you at this time. Your angels and guides send you 333 to know and be assured that these 'new' guides may be different and will assist you in gaining very specific knowledge. In meditation, famous scientists, teachers, philosophers, and gurus may send you messages and information or downloads. You will be able to understand and assimilate their teachings.

With 333 floating around, your guides may be indicating that a period of growth is coming to a close. Don't be alarmed. What comes next is the reaping of what you've sown and nurtured. The angels want you to consider the seasons of the year. You've just completed a spring and summer cycle. Now is the fall and soon you can rest in the winter, gathering new ideas and opportunities to power your next growth phase forward. But for now, your angels would like you to begin slowing the pace, chilling and relaxing more than pushing forward. Enjoy your accomplishments.

3333

Someone may see you as an earth angel at this time, or decide to name you their mentor. With the doubling of the master number 33, your spirituality, and connection to source or spirit, is strong and secure. Material and the mundane may not interest you much. The angels are reminding you with 3333 that while it's wonderful and blissful hanging out in the high vibes and dimensions, you have work to do in the collective or for the world. It's time to ground yourself without fear of missing out of accidentally losing your connection to the higher vibrations and dimensions. Someone, somewhere, needs your guidance, your insight, and your problem-solving abilities.

The angels and guides also want you to know that should you feel compelled to establish a humanitarian project, however big or small, it will be a success.

Chapter 10:

Angel Numbers With Recurring Fours

Four is stable. Four is practical. Four doesn't waste time and gets down to business. Number four is also an indicator of trustworthiness and a firm foundation or structure. Four also represents steady growth and, for some, the pinnacle of a goal achieved.

Recurring fours anchor their neighboring digits in reality and reassure that the foundations remain rock solid for as long as they need to serve you.

Core Number Four

The appearance of four throughout your day carries the message that all is well and stable. Someone or the situation remains unshakeable and solid. The carpet will not be pulled out from under you.

If times have been hectic and you have been neglecting yourself, your guides and angels may send you fours to announce that it's safe for you to slow down, chill, relax, and be at ease so you can enjoy what you've built and achieved.

If you are stressing and fearing that you're making no progress, fours appear to encourage you to persevere. Your angels and guides are working on the matter with you, and a breakthrough will occur in only a matter of time.

Angels and guides send you fours and sequences of fours when your career is about to accelerate in a positive direction. They're nudging you to be prepared, value your skills, organize or reorganize your life and lifestyle for greatest efficiency, and to recognize your worth and ability to complete even the toughest projects.

If you've been praying for help, fours may announce that a professional or a wise and canny advisor is here to aid you.

Feeling betrayed or burned in love or business? Your angel guides and messages will give you the heads up that someone will be gentle, trustworthy, and dependable by linking them to the number four.

Fours also signal good news about your home, rentals, accommodation, and similar concerns. Finding a roommate, housemate, or moving in with your partner is also signaled by a parade of Fours through your environment.

When the angels want to gently remind you that you're holding onto something you should let go of, they may also send a four or series of fours. This may be for those cases when you know a change is imminent or needed, but you don't want to leave your comfort zone.

44

You may best achieve the stability you seek this time with the help of someone close to you. Together you achieve more and enhance each other's positive traits and abilities. This may be your life partner, your business partner, a room or housemate, or even a pet with a similar temperament to you.

When you see 44s around the time you're looking for a new home, the angels are letting you know that that specific location will be good to boost your career or help you hold a part-time job.

In terms of investments, 44s are your guides' way of saying, "This has long-term potential but once invested you're committed for the full term." If you're considering two retirement or investment options for your long-term financial stability, the parade of 44s may be advising you to place equal amounts in each option. A trustworthy advisor may also be confirmed as such by the random appearances of 44 in their presence. It could be that menu item 44 is on special at the place you dine, or that your watch showed 10:44 when you walked into their office.

If you've had a period of ill-health, 44 may be sent to reassure you the worst is over. Your condition is stable and healthy, and likely to be so for a while. If you've undergone a procedure, you may need another within a certain period. Your angels want you to know that you'll recover very well.

If you're seeking an equal marriage based on more than only attraction, the path may be paved with 44s! The angels are letting you know that your marriage or life partnership will be stable in every way with little conflict and great teamwork. Together, you and your partner will build a wonderful life and relationship together as you both approach the relationship from a mature perspective.

444

With 444, the angels are asking you why you're so bored. You've gotten exactly what you've asked for in terms of security, safety and good finances. Life is good, so why are you not content? You may be guided to review and reflect on your life. Why do you feel a piece is missing? Why do you crave something new, or some kind of excitement? When you're ready, your guides and angels will arrange for your next challenge so you can figure this out.

444 may also mean an unchanging cycle. You and your partner or friend may be having the same conversation over and over again, yet neither of you is satisfied or can find something else to talk about. Your guides want you to know you're in your comfort zone and that it may grow toxic if you don't try something a little different. It's a good time to take up an online course or share a new leisurely pursuit with your partner or friend.

Triple fours may also indicate that you'll be hard at work for some time. Leave and vacation may be delayed or canceled. Your angels want you to know that the effort will serve you well, securing your foundation even more. They are also encouraging you to put away any extra money for your future reward or for a rainy day.

Seeing 444 every few minutes may be the angels observing your stubbornness on an issue and encouraging you to meet someone halfway. There's a stalemate until you do. There will be no winners, only losers if you aren't willing to negotiate or redefine. They don't want you to miss an opportunity over hard-headedness.

If you've been stuck or feel that obstacles meet you at every time, your guides and angels are advising you to look at what lies beneath those obstacles. Can you change your perspective, while you're at it? Addressing root problems now clears the way forward for now and the future, too.

4444

A new cycle of life-long stability or knowledge is here. What you gain now should stick with you for a lifetime. Your angels and guides are encouraging you to maintain only healthy habits at this time so you carry them on into your stable period. You may be graduating, doing a course on a practical skill or going through a process of understanding yourself and those around you. These insights will shape and hold your future.

When 4444 appears around you, know that you are surrounded by people who are bound by their words. Promises will be kept, contracts honored to the letter. You cannot renegotiate in the future. You cannot leave this relationship. It is binding. This is a good sign for a lifelong, through-thick-and-thin type of marriage.

The angels and guides also want you to know that they are flagging anything and anyone who may endanger your foundations at this time. They will give you signs, angel numbers or and more, should someone or something threaten your home, possessions, or wellbeing. They have your back. It's okay for you to relax or let your guard down from time to time.

When 4444 appears at the end of a cycle, at work or in a relationship, you may have reached a pinnacle or glass ceiling. Your guides and angels are communicating that this is as far as you can go or build in this situation. Sticking to this job can bring you little expansion to your role or another promotion. Alternatively, your love for a person or pet is at its height and will remain so. For those seeking to make something work that isn't meant to be, or who have persevered believing a sinking ship can still sail, your angels and guides are telling you it's time to abandon this venture or place and find a new route forward.

Chapter 11:

Angel Numbers With Recurring Fives

While three creates change, five indicates that change is here and cannot be avoided. Five challenges you to expand, to take your eyes off the screen and realize there are wider horizons available to you. Five reminds you of your pioneering spirit from one, and prods you to take up your next adventure.

Five is also a number of versatility, of sharp observation, and the seeking of knowledge.

Recurring fives modify and challenge the numbers grouped with them to embrace change.

Core Number Five

The appearance of a plethora of the number fives in your life rings in changes and expansion. The angels are letting you know the green light is here for travel, study, or a new hobby. Whatever expands your minds, breathens your experience, strengthens your sense of self, and challenges you to look deeper into your soul would make an excellent use of your time now. In fact, the angels may smile at how quickly you may shrug off "wastes of time" and almost single-mindedly seek knowledge. Without this knowledge, positive change may not last long.

With the dance of Fives through your day, your guides and angels are bringing Freedom to your attention. Do you feel sufficiently free to express yourself, to move as you wish? This message may come when you feel most restricted by life or circumstances. The angels may wish you to reassess your sense of freedom. Is it illusionary? Does it need to be redefined? Does the 9-to-5 job truly satisfy you or do you feel smothered by the routine? Do your material assets and obligations chain you to a lifestyle that stifles you? Are you in an environment where you feel free to talk, to create, to be yourself? If not, can you move yourself to an environment that feels freer, or adapt to a new mindset?

Through showing you instances of fives, the angels may be cautioning you that your current actions or beliefs are creating a mental, spiritual, or emotional cage around you. Again, they remind you to choose wisely those options and paths that ensure you have a degree of freedom that feeds your soul.

If you're wondering at your sense of restlessness, five's message from your guides is that it's time to seek new horizons and adventures. Exploring, even if you don't leave your sofa, will satisfy your thirst for adventure. And if you should see a fare with fives advertised by a travel agent, event organizer, or short course, it may be a good idea to take up the offer or a similar one!

With fives prancing around your world, a stream of ideas and exciting projects may flitter through your mind. The angels and guides advise you to stay grounded in order to better assess and explore these wonderful thoughts and ideas. This is the main challenge of five: to get out of your head and ground yourself along with the best of those ideas.

55

Major life changes are on the way. Don't worry. You've got this. You angels want you to know you've been through similarly large changes before. Use the lessons you learned then to make this an easier transition.

With 55s popping up frequently, you angels may be trying to help you reach a decision regarding two choices by indicating that both choices are equally good and will not delay or negatively impact your spiritual journey.

When 55s appear during times of stress, your angels are reminding you that the situation can be easily changed through choosing to be more positive, anticipate the silver lining and to work with them to bring a change in the situation sooner by adapting to the changes and treating others as you wish to be treated.

Your angels are also giving you a high-five! Well done! They are happy with all you're doing to transition. They will continue aiding you with your goals and spiritual growth. Keep doing what you're doing and look for the synchronicities and angel numbers that they will send you.

555

You're about to step into a period of significant changes. The changes may occur concurrently or in a series. If you're feeling overwhelmed, ask for assistance and the intensity will ease.

Your angels and guides want you to know that the easiest way forward is by letting things go. By refusing to let go you're denying space for growth and positive change. You may need to release material things, emotional issues, or even granting forgiveness to others and to yourself. Choose what you love and love what you choose.

Something or someone you thought you'd left behind may reappear or become important to you again. Try not to hold onto it or them too tightly. Whatever is meant to remain with you will do so. Release what no longer serves you and them.

You and everything around you is in a state of change. Matters will twist and turn quickly and you'll need to act with positivity, compassion, and decisiveness. Deal with what is directly in front of you before attempting to guess on and prepare for an outcome. Let love and compassion be your compass.

For lightworkers and others sensitive to energy shifts, you may be confounded by timeline shifts and sudden energetic shifts that may be challenging to process and integrate. Ground and visualize in the highest timeline available to you.

5555

This number is a sign that wonderful things will flow into your life. This also confirms you are in an environment of positive vibrations. With 5555 around, your guides want you to know that they appreciate you and all the positive energy you share.

5-D and higher messages may be streamed to you, carrying glimpses of possible futures. You don't need to hold onto any of them, your guides want you to know. These are mere possibilities and are meant to inspire you.

You're at the end of seemingly interminable changes. Stability is not far off. Life will soon be more settled and you will have plenty of time to appreciate what you've achieved, rest, and enjoy the love and joy that surrounds you.

Any new health regime, especially ones that allow for variety and flexibility, will benefit you well. You will be able to continue with this exercise or diet change even if your circumstances change. This new healthy habit will be adaptable to any of your life changes, so invest in yourself and your health.

The angels want you to know this person or situation will be constantly and often rapidly changing. You may need to be someone's anchor at this time.

If you have a partnership question in mind, the 5555s are a confirmation that you and your partner are aligned or of the same mind about any impending changes. Both of you are implementing changes towards the same goal or seeking similar changes to your environment or lifestyle. Your decisions for change will be harmonious and easy to adjust to. Any difficulties during the transition will see both of you working as a team to overcome. Working together to make these changes happen smoothly and efficiently strengthens your foundations and belief in each other. Your guides and their guides and ancestors are cheering each milestone at this time.

Chapter 12:

Angel Numbers With Recurring Sixes

At the heart of six lies protection and nurturing, ringed by compassion and understanding. Six prioritizes others, sometimes to its detriment, often to the betterment of all. Six is the number of generosity and reciprocity. Six a hug from the universe.

Recurring sixes amplify and modify the meaning of the numbers surrounding it, tempering them with compassion and altruism.

Core Number Six

When sixes begin miraculously materializing around you, your angels and guides are indicating that love is all around you. Not only that, but the love you're sending out and showing to the world is being returned many times over.

If you have an idea or person in mind when six strikes you as significant, the angels are confirming that the idea or person needs your nurturing or protection. During this period, if you're feeling lonely or loveless, or even childless, the angels and guides will announce that a person, an animal, a plant, or even a region, is entering your life—one that you can love and nurture, or parent.

At times, six can indicate that a sacrifice may be needed on your part. You may need to give your time or a gift to another, or to a cause that supports your community or people in distress. The angels assure you, that in your time of need, you too will receive at least as much as you give. Sometimes sixes are sent to remind you that you're sacrificing too much for too little. You may be allowing a situation that isn't balanced with equal give-and-take to flourish.

Acceptance is around you when your guides send you instances of six. If you're feeling a pariah, self-conscious, judged, or even ashamed, your guides are assuring you that despite what you may feel, you are accepted and loved for who you are, just as you are. At times, they may also remind you via sixes that you need to accept and love yourself as you are. You are a beautiful being whose light and good heart illuminates, protects, and comforts those in your circle. Never doubt that.

Angels and guides may send you a series of sixes to confirm your wisdom and ability to counsel others. This is particularly true for healers and lightworkers. Now is not the time to second guess yourself. Accept your wisdom and use it responsibly.

With six resonating with beauty, harmony, and art, any concerns and questions about beautifying your environment get a resounding yes from your angels and guides. It's time to refurbish, replant, renovate, or create what brings you joy and harmony. Your ability to harmoniously arrange your space is very high. Doing so will raise the vibration of the entire place and the people around you.

66

You need to reaffirm your faith and trust in the universe. If you feel you're stuck in a loveless place, finding it hard to connect to others, your angels are letting you know that a little faith in them and trust in the process will allow them to more easily bring what you desire to you. With 66, your guides want you to know that what you're manifesting is already en route to you. It will reach you as soon as you get out of your own way.

When there's a need to balance the spiritual and material in your life, your angels and guides might send you 66. You may be working too hard, being overly materialistic, lapsing in spiritual practices that help center and ground you, or are trying too hard to compete with the Joneses. Your angels are suggesting you recalibrate your priorities to what makes you feel happy and fulfilled over the long-term; to what feeds your soul and brings more balance in your life.

With 66, the angels are showing you that it's safe to expand in a direction that helps nurture your community. Such projects will quickly gather momentum and support.

For some, 66 could also indicate a baby: a child, furbaby, or even a long-term project that may take you many years to complete. You will learn to nurture, to compromise, and to express love and affection during the process.

66 reveals harmony is coming into your life. You may work well with others now, or find common ground with those who might have antagonized you before. Harmony will allow for mutual expansion and abundance, so it's worth seeking and working for it now in all areas of your life.

666

You still have some work to do to improve your life. Obsessions or addictions are holding you back from true happiness and fulfillment. Whether it's binge-watching the newest reality TV shows, overindulging in alcohol or drugs, dreaming of a life with someone who could never be yours, or obsessing over your image and social media, your angels and guides would like you to take a step back, take a deep breath, and ask yourself if focusing your energy on all or one of these truly leading you to greater happiness? If not, your guides and angels are waiting for you to let them know to support you and bring in any help you may need to find a healthy, balanced way forward to true happiness.

Over-committing could also be signaled by 666. Are you spreading yourself too thin, being the people-pleaser, feeling guilty to say no? Your angels and guides would like you to know that it's okay to say no sometimes; that you aren't obliged to ensure everyone else is happy except for yourself. Try saying no once or twice or asking for help.

If you're afraid of missing out on something in a Cinderella way, your angels and guides will be your fairy godmother and either help you get that experience or send something even better your way!

Giving your power away! 666 will be the angels call to you to let you know when you're allowing others to dictate to you unfairly. Whether it's a pushy salesperson, a friend who always says they know what's best for you but don't, a guilt-tripping parent, or your pet; your guides and angels are letting you know you're in danger of receiving the short end of the stick and need to retain your power or speak out. You are an individual. You have power. You may need to use it!

With 666s floating around, your guides and angels are letting you know that money and success lie in your palm. You will need to manage both well. In some ways, they're letting you know that this is a test or exam along your path that will determine your next lesson. Enjoy your material wealth, but manage it well and with responsibility.

With 666 popping up around certain conversations and locations, your angels and guides are wagging their fingers at you. Your attitude or prevailing energy may be one of entitlement, arrogance, or narcissism. They would like you to take a reality check. Similarly, you may be admiring and wishing to be like someone who displays these traits. Your guides and angels want you to know that you don't need to be like them. You have a beautiful spirit, loving and compassionate, which are much more valued traits.

6666

The angels recognize the brimming compassion and love you hold and how you can help others significantly by sharing with them. Amplify the positive aspects of your life by making small changes.

Your angels are singing your praises with 6666! You've passed difficult tests, faced dilemmas and temptations with grace, and helped others recover their connection to love and compassion. You may receive many affirmations from your circle and community at this time. Any sacrifices you've made will be acknowledged and appreciated at this time.

Your high, loving vibe and zest for life is inspiring not just to people, but animals and other creatures too! Dogs and cats will adore you, wanting to stay in your energy field, children will want your hugs or to hold your hand, plants will grow healthy and strong around you, and wherever you go, harmony and calm will follow. As long as you can retain your balance and joy in life, this high vibe will continue. Should you lose it, this vibration will be more easily attained.

You may feel deeply emotional and empathic to all of those around you. You may need to retreat to a quiet, peaceful location or meditate at this time. Your intuition and empathy are extremely strong and so are your sensitivities. You may also develop temporary allergies to synthetic scents and other non-natural products. Rest, relax, and allow yourself to readjust to yourself. Grounding exercises will help at this time. If you're going out or are around people, put up some psychic protection or ask your guides and angels to help you keep your energy purely your own.

You have access to healing energies and intuitive knowledge at this time. Your angels and guides would like you to explore them further. They will send you additional signs about these healing modalities. For your own healing, sound, and listening are most important. It's time to revise your playlists. Listen only to music that makes you feel happier.

The angels applaud you. You have mastered some difficult emotions and have learned not to suppress them, or vent them hurtfully. You can process and flow with your emotions with ease. Your creativity will help you express yourself without words.

Chapter 13:

Angel Numbers With Recurring Sevens

Seven has a reputation of being mystical, spiritual, and extremely wise. Yet, it is also the number of secrecy, the hidden, the unseen. This mysterious number is linked to fortune, growth, higher thought, and maybe being just a little spacey at times!

Sevens impart greater spiritual and fortuitous gravity to the numbers around them. Sometimes, they may indicate that there is a deeper meaning you'll have to seek.

Core Number Seven

Sevens floating around your environment are often sent to you when your angels and guides begin preparing you for the next phase in your mental or spiritual development. Research is vital for your next steps in healthy growth. Religion, traditional lore, or culture may inspire you. A variety of spiritual teachings and theories may refine your own personal views and beliefs about the universe. It is a good time to question and seek answers. Those who are sensitive and psychic may receive new spiritual guides and angels to work with them. You may be guided to esoteric knowledge and practices that may aid you at this time. In addition, you may be called to take up or treasure traditional and ancient knowledge and practices.

Sevens are also employed by your angels and guides to underscore important bits of wisdom sent to you, or that you should record your thoughts as they may be quite profound and revelatory. Sharing these thoughts may help others at this time.

When your latent healing abilities have grown to the point of being of use to the collective, your angels and guides may send you sevens. They are encouraging you to explore your healing abilities. These healing abilities may include listening and writing.

When sevens are sent to you, it's time to begin digging deeper into truths. Hidden or lost things will be found. Secrets may resurface or be exposed. The true natures of those close to you will be seen, and you may be able to discern the unseen. Psychic and emotional growth will accelerate and you will need your research to guide you. Ground yourself and proceed cautiously. Your thirst for knowledge may prove obsessive, so ensure you exercise self-discipline.

The angels send you comfort when you see sevens during times when you feel hidden enemies are working against you. They assure you that any wrongdoing against you will be exposed, and you or your loved one will be vindicated.

Angels and guides may playfully send you sevens when good fortune and magic abounds. The sight of a seven may confirm a wish you've just made, or that your fortune is changing for the better. They remind you to be of good heart, use your knowledge wisely, and playfully create your experience.

77

Congratulations! Your luck is changing! Your angels and guides want you to know that while it may seem that way to you and people around you, the reality is you're working hard for the good that's flowing to you. Whether it was applying your wisdom at difficult times, following your intuition, or even the positive vibes that you're sending out into the world, you'll now achieve and joy all that's due to you!

The sudden appearance of 77 may be an indication that you should change your mind over a choice to bring in more success and stability. If you receive a windfall, your guides and angels may advise you to invest that money wisely or to put it into paying off a debt like your home bond. This will double your fortune over the longer term.

77 may indicate that in spiritual matters you may feel conflicted or that you have to choose between two spiritual schools or religious teachings. Your angels and guides are pointing out that there's no need to stress. You don't actually need to make a choice. Both options can work together to help you attain that greater spiritual understanding that you're seeking. In most cases, you may discern the truth because both, and other schools of belief, share the same basic wisdom.

Your angels and guides are confirming that your psychic and energetic abilities are growing at a fast rate. You might find a friend or a new mentor or guru soon to help you explore your expanding abilities.

77 also signals a deeper connection to the natural world. You may feel a stronger bond with animals and plants, and feel called to help them in some way. With 77, you may have mystical and miraculous interactions

with animals and nature. Finding a beautiful nature location that fills your souls, allowing you the peace and space to explore your expanding spiritual insight is close by.

777

The rewards for your efforts are here. Your angels and guides want you to know through 777 that what you envisioned and worked so hard for is now here. It's time to relax. You can enjoy your rewards with ease and grace!

Through 777 your angels are letting you know that you've gained an A+ in manifesting! You have mastered the tools and mindset required to manifest and create. Now, apply your wisdom to ensure you only manifest what's healthy for you. Your angels and guides are trusting you to use your gifts responsibly.

With 777 floating around, your angels and guides want you to know that they'll soon be sharing little-known knowledge with you. This knowledge may be very relevant to your life purpose and future success even though it may make little sense to you at present. Hold on to this knowledge that they'll send you. In a little while or a few years, it will all make sense.

Sometimes, with 777 around, you may become a temporary safe-keeper for some object or piece of information that is part of a universal whole. You may find a crystal or other object that you have to hold in safe-keeping until you meet the person for whom it's meant. When you meet that person, your guides and their guides will prompt you to gift or exchange the item you safe-kept. Other times, you may travel with the item so as to set it in the location it's most needed or return it to its home to rest. Your guides will help you know where to take it and what to do with it at the location. In this way, you are physically helping the angels and your guides. Often, if you're not hearing or heeding the message, the item will inexplicably disappear as it returns home or to the location where it's meant to be.

7777

Despite events in the collective energies or what appears around you, stay optimistic and hopeful. Help raise the vibration at this time and let love rule.

A new spiritual way of being is available to you. You've done all the hard work. Now, all that remains is to choose your path forward. The new beginning will be easier for you to assimilate and adapt to. The lessons left for you are of the highest order.

With 7777 floating around, your angels and guides may be guiding you to undertake a pilgrimage to a sacred place. Everything will be arranged miraculously and you'll experience something that is meant uniquely for you at this sacred place.

What's your secret? is something you may hear as often as you see 7777. Your life is so aligned and blessed that many will be wanting to know how you attained such peace and prosperity. Your angels and guides bring you the message that others will want to learn your secret and be talking about you.

Chapter 14:

Angel Numbers With Recurring Eights

Infinity. Circles. Mastery. These are all aspects of number eight. So is materialism, financial and social success, as well as logic and long-term planning. Eights indicate quick, focused energy although some of it may be internal.

Eights lend their material and success vibrations to numbers surrounding them, amplifying similar attributes.

Core Number Eight

The materializing of eights throughout your day may signal that you may be called to speak in public or deliver a speech, report, or demonstration. Your angels and guides wish you to know that they will stand beside you and guide you through it, should you wish their help. The presentation is sure to go smoothly. Request their help with technical matters such as sound and vision so you can focus on presenting at your best. At this time, they also wish you to know that your speech and writing are inspirational and will strike a chord with many.

If you fear for your job safety or request guidance on earning more than you currently do, your angels and guides may indicate the path to success via eights and sequences of eights. As with public speaking, there's no need to be nervous during interviews and performance evaluations. At times, when you're contemplating becoming your own boss or networking, the appearance of eights is an angelic thumbs up!

When it feels like you're moving through sludge in your daily life, your angelic team will send you eight as a sign that determination will see you through this temporary slow down. Faster progress isn't far off, and what progress you're currently making is commendable so keep up the good work!

As the sign for infinity, angels may send you eights when a significant karmic cycle is beginning again. You may have the option of ascending through or transcending an issue that has held you back for years, or even lifetimes. Pay attention to your intuition, your dreams, and other messages, or ask the angels and guides in mediation for help in ending the cycle—or for a healing—so all concerned can move forward with freedom and love.

When you've asked for financial aid or relief, money flowing in or arriving unexpectedly will be announced by eights. The angels wish you to accept this gift and use it wisely. The financing of large ticket items, housing, or vehicles may be offered in surprising ways. At this time, you're unlikely to lose money or choose bad investments.

88

Financial abundance is here for you. If you find it hard to accept financial abundance and monetary rewards without struggle, your angels and guides want you to know that you deserve the money and rewards coming in to ease your burdens. It's okay for you to enjoy your financial abundance. There's no need to feel guilt. Rather, your angels would like to help you heal any blockages that prevent you from accepting this abundance or which cause you to self-sabotage when you do receive prosperity.

Your financial wellbeing and future prospects are being worked on by your angels and guides when you see 88. They may mark doors of opportunity or helpful people, and they will ensure that you have all the information to make wise and profitable choices.

A merger in business or love may be around the corner when 88 is presented to you. While the offers may be tempting, your angels wish you to keep in mind that you are equal in worth, acumen, and ability to the ones making the offers, and that you are not obliged to accept anything if you're happy being as you are. Listen carefully at this time as they'll alert you to anyone who doesn't have your best interests at heart.

With 88 appearing, anything that may have been delayed or put on hold will now be prioritized again. Progress will be swift, aided by your angels' wings.

When 88 appears during a challenging period, your angels and guides are asking you to remain balanced and seek fairness. You can stand above petty grievances. What matters is your reaction and behavior, not others, because universal justice or karma is at play.

888

Send gratitude to the universe for all the good in your life and around you. Everything is happening according to divine timing and your divine path. Once again, you are reminded of balance and compassion.

When triple-8s play peek-a-boo with you, your angels and guides are reminding you that there's no need to compare yourself with any others. You are beautiful and unique, achieving what you need to in this lifetime. You don't need to prove yourself or your status to anyone. You have all that you need and so much more. Shiny things may look great, but not at the expense of the true treasures of your life—your love, family, and friends.

Your angels and guide send you 888 to congratulate you on mastering material life. Whether this means you're surrounded by luxury or prefer the minimalist approach to life, they are pleased with your management of the material aspects of life. They are now working on sending you an abundance of what you next need be it time, space, or a change of view. For confirmed bachelors and bachelorettes, a major love may enter to add some missing element to your life.

For some, 888 is sent to notify you that energies in your life—especially lower vibrations that may sabotage love, success, or mastery—are transmuting or transforming into a higher vibration or expression of yourself. Expect to meet new people who match your vibration or who are in the same process of transmuting energies. Other acquaintances and even friends may fade away at this time.

8888

With 8888, your guides and angels are reminding you of the flow of energy and interconnectedness of all things. You are now that butterfly who can cause a storm or change fortunes for others. Keep in mind consequences, good and bad, before committing to anything or anyone, particularly in commerce, corporate spending, and the environment. The same can be said for your relationships. Pay special attention to your children and pets and the greatest consequences may be felt by them.

For some, energy healing abilities may be awakened. You may choose to get energy healing at this time or even study modalities for yourself. Each session will attune you even more to your place and purpose energetically.

8888 may also be sent as encouragement and confirmation that it's time for further study. This may be for your own interest or to attain your next leadership role. Whatever the course, you have the skills, drive, and attitude to succeed in your studies, too. You may also need to study or re-train as new technology or a new process of working may be changing your industry. Keep abreast of the latest news and developments to maintain your knowledge.

The angels are cheering you. You've reached a major life goal, possibly sooner than expected. This may leave a vacuum in your life and your guides are asking you to reassess your direction and set a new goal or two. Alternatively, if you need a rest, the angels are guiding you to consider whether this change of pace suits you permanently or makes you happier. You may now have the option of working remotely, emigrating to a locale you've always dreamed of, or setting a faster pace by reaching for your next goal.

When 8888 comes around often, your guides and angels are urging you to count your personal successes and not discount them. Success in life depends on personal successes, too. So, if you've quit smoking, quit sugar, are getting more exercise, or are rebuilding personal relationships, well done! Your angels want you to know that your success is well-rounded and will lead to an even more rewarding phase in your life.

Chapter 15:

Angel Numbers With Recurring Nines

Number nine celebrates courage, cautions against excessive perfectionism, and carries the banner for worthwhile humanitarian and environmental causes. Nines urges speech against intolerance, injustice, and apathy. As the last single digit, nine carries an urgency to complete a task and to complete it well!

Within a sequence, nines amplify and encourage the positive attributes of other numbers.

Core Number Nines

By planting bold nines throughout your day, your angels and guides are signaling that the end to your project or lesson is nearing. In just a short time, you will reach completion, but you must persevere at this time. Never give up. There is more than hope at this time.

With the appearance of nines, your celestial team is cheering your courage and urging you to proceed despite any fears you may hold. If you're in an abusive relationship at home or at work, they will help you speak out and find a positive, safe way forward. Let "Be Dauntless" be your motto.

Feeling impulsive or reckless? Your angels send you nines to urge you to reconsider. This may not be the best way forward. Your solution may cause more harm than good or this is not the time for it. They will show you a better way or better time. Stay tuned in for their next message to you.

Is your perfectionism hurting you or others? This is another message your angels may want you to contemplate at this time. It's a good time to research Wabi Sabi, or take a break. Your closeness to a project and focusing on tiny details may subtract from the beauty of what you've created so far. Furthermore, the time you spend on your work or craft may be better spent with friends and family. It's time to lighten up and have some fun!

Another message of a series of nines may relate to honesty. If you've asked for confirmation regarding a person's or institution's honesty, the angels will confirm with the materialization of a nine. If you're recovering from a betrayal, they indicate those who won't abuse your trust or privacy by linking them with a significant nine. Alternatively, if you are in a period of great self-growth or experiencing a dark night of the soul, a succession of nines suggests you reflect on yourself with deep honesty. It may be painful, but it is the healing you need at this time.

By gifting you a nine, your angels and guides want you to know that this is not the time to pursue money or material gain. It's the time to honor yourself, your ideals, the beauty and diversity around you, and the wealth of your experience. This, too, takes courage and generosity of spirit.

99

With the wisdom you've gained, it's time to revise your long-term goals. Accept your leadership skills. It's also time to hone your talents. Your angels are notifying you that this time is preparation for the next phase in your life.

You're on the last step of realizing a dream or have just achieved it. This achievement will change your life, though maybe not exactly as envisioned. Your angels and guides want you to know that regardless, the changes resulting will bring you prestige as well as recognition from society.

Life is sweet. Enjoy the simple pleasures in life during this hectic, crazy time. Your angels would love to accompany you to the beach or gardens where you can breathe deep, dig your toes in the sand and just be yourself for a few minutes. Being busy is exhausting and what you're achieving is good, but these time-out moments will enrich your life immeasurably. Appreciate with a child-like view, all the delight around you.

You don't have long to wait for your news. The message has already been sent. You angels and guides are reminding you to look at your messages from institutions at this time. The message will change your future direction almost immediately.

Your creativity is moving onto the next level. You will master a new technique or application that will significantly improve your finances and stability, freeing time for you to experiment even more with your creative endeavors. Keep going with that creative streak!

Listen to that song! With 99 floating around, your angels and guides are letting you know that what you're listening to at that moment is highly significant. If it's music, pay attention to how the song makes you feel. More messages may come from the title or song lyrics.

999

You are applauded for your good heart and hard-won experience. Not just your angels, but everyone around you does too. Your sacrifice is talked about and will be remembered. Your community work may bring you fame or a higher profile that will allow you to be even more effective in your community goals. Remain humble and show gratitude for this good fortune but don't try to hide from the spotlight. Your community needs your voice and leadership at this time.

When 999 appears, your angels and guides may be referring to a karmic relationship that is changing because it's been healed. Your friends or love may remain in your life, but the karmic tie is dissolved. You may drift apart, or find that the unburdened relationship is now lighter, healthier, and more fun than before.

Similarly, 999 may indicate that a new karmic relationship will soon begin. This could be with a love, a business colleague, or even a spiritual teacher. Your angels and guides would like you to know that you have the wisdom and compassion to dissolve this karma without undue drama and trauma to you both. During your interactions with this person, you will always maintain a clear perspective and empathy, but neither will you let this relationship affect your personal power. This relationship carries the potential to grant you more personal wisdom by analyzing your responses to this person and preventing codependency.

9999

New opportunities and blessings are headed your way. Be prepared to receive them. Don't be overwhelmed by the magnitude of these opportunities. Your angels and guides are affirming their faith in you to carry any of these opportunities through to completion.

You hold everything you need within you! No need to wait for help or a special time, it's all achievable now! Your angels and guides are confirming you have the strengths, the vision, the ability, and the knowledge that you need to successfully begin and complete a project or process. You don't need anyone to hold your hand or direct you. Follow your inner guidance, take the unique or eccentric path, and make this all happen on your own. You've more than "got this"!

Chapter 16:

Angel Numbers With Recurring Zeros

Sometimes referred to as the Egg, zero holds ultimate potential in every way. Like eight, it signals a cycle beginning or ending. Zero is also linked to spirituality, god, and universal creation.

From Taoists to Christians to Mathematicians, the power of zero is apart from any other numeral. It speaks of humility yet also creation. It renders all differences obsolete while placing all who encounter it on the same level. Zero is a hero, potentially.

Zero is the ultimate amplifying digit, multiplying the power of the numbers that surround it.

Core Number Zero

While some see zero as carrying no message from your angels or guides, its presence is usually more remarkable than most other digits, underlining that your potential is unlimited and your connection to spirit and universal law is strong.

When you're feeling empty or in despair that you've lost everything and are unable to pick up the pieces, angels and guides send zero as a reminder that you have the wonderful opportunity to start over unencumbered by the past. They ask you to see the situation as liberating, to take comfort that with this unlimited potential anything is possible!

A succession of zeros dotting your day may be a gentle reminder that you may be thinking too small. Are you unaware of or denying your own potential? Are you dismissing a great opportunity because you're discounting the potential? Keep in mind that great potential often takes time to materialize or be realized. You may need to commit to helping realize your own or another's potential. This is especially true for creative endeavors and growth.

Being ringed by zeros may also indicate that you need to look at your life and goals holistically. Focusing overly on one area, such as your career, could be causing an imbalance that affects other areas of your life negatively. Putting more effort or equal energy to a neglected area of your life at this time could realign you to your easier, healthiest path.

Through zero, your angels are announcing accelerated growth is possible in all areas of your life if you are prepared to put in the work. You may be able to "skip levels" in your spiritual, academic, or emotional growth.

If you're returning to school or feel self-conscious, the appearance of zeros assures you that you have no need to feel out of place. No one is better than the other. All of you contain the same potential to succeed. All that is left is for you to put in consistent work through each cycle—daily, weekly, monthly—until your goal is reached.

00

Two opportunities for renewal, rebirth, or new beginnings are here. You may experience a new beginning jointly with a renewal of some form.

There may be a crucial element you're ignoring in your life. Are you paying attention to your health and nutrition? Are you paying enough attention to your loved ones? Are you expressing yourself and allowing happiness into your life? If not, your angels and guides would like to help you find that crucial element that will enrich your life.

The messages of adjoining digits are doubly amplified.

000

You're on a deadline. Your angels and guides want you to know that you're on a special universal deadline and have this unique once-in-a-lifetime opportunity to accelerate your growth or achieve a lifetime goal. If you choose not to accept this deadline, that's okay, too.

Others around you are also in the process of going through new beginnings. If you work together to co-create, you will all achieve a greater whole. Collaborations and community teamwork is changing everyone's reality for the better.

So many possibilities are offered to you at this time. You angels and guides would like to remind you of your spiritual and affectionate connections to certain people or certain locations in the world as this can aid with your decision-making.

Dimensional shifts and bouncing around different timelines may confuse you. Your angels and guys offer to help ground you. You may need to ground more often than normal.

A situation is resetting. Your angels want you to know that you can start with a clean slate. It's time to write a new story without any baggage from the past. Second chances in relationships or your career are here should you wish to accept them.

The meaning of the messages from the numbers next to 000s are tripled.

0000

Limitlessness is here! Restricting your thoughts, ideas, and emotions serves no purpose. Reach beyond the stars as anything and everything is possible! So, be careful what you wish for!

You mastered something you'd thought was impossible. Now, you can do the action or go through the process with little or no effort. Your angels and guides are well pleased with you.

Bliss is easy to achieve as your vibrations raise even higher. You may find yourself slipping into bliss while meditating or just relaxing, or even admiring nature. Bless will become a more frequent feeling in your life. Your angels and guides would like you to enjoy the experiences!

You've achieved your life's purpose. Your karmic debts are all paid. It's time now for you to create what your soul desires to leave as a legacy to others. This is your next great work that may take the rest of your lifetime. It may merge all that you're passionate about and help others also find new beginnings and soul expression.

Chapter 17:

Greatly Significant Angel Numbers

Some angel numbers are more prominently known than others, either because they're seen and discussed more widely, or because they tend to appear during perceived significant times. These numbers are visually simpler with mirrored or repeating digits; many of them seen on digital clocks and readouts. It could also be that these angel numbers are considered 'more' special because it's believed they precede a wish coming true, greater financial or other success, a major life partner entering your life, or even magically bestow wishes on you!

This list of greatly significant numbers is only the tip of a very large iceberg when it comes to the angelic messages being sent to you. I recommend looking up the meaning of these numbers under the various categories as well, so you can discern the strongest angel message for you at this time. Still, if you spot a number and feel a wish is yours, wish away!

1000 (10:00)

An exceptional new beginning is here. You may be able to fulfill a long-held life goal or even one that you've been waiting lifetimes to achieve. This new beginning is occurring in divine timing and may seem erratic in the time it takes to completely establish you in the new situation.

1010 (10:10)

You're doing great! Keep going!

Another message of 10:10 is that you're in the final steps of preparation on something you've been working on for a long time. It may be personal or in the work sphere, but whatever it is, your angels want you to know that soon, you'll be sitting in the place you've been dreaming of for so long.

1111 (11:11)

An exclamation point that your spiritual awakening is here, or that your spiritual journey will once again take priority over other aspects of your life. Your angels and guides are with you every step of the way.

Your intuition is your superpower! Follow it! Your angels and guides and Higher Self are sending you oodles of information on all that you ask. It's more than a feeling. Go with the feeling.

While some joyfully make a wish at the sight of this number, the message is that your manifesting energy is at a peak and the universe is likely to accommodate any of your requests at this time. So, go ahead and wish, but wish wisely!

For twin flame and life-partner messages, see Chapter 3.

1122 (11:22)

You're in a wonderful cycle of building and boosting your finances and spiritual growth. Keep following your intuition, learning, and experimenting! You can attain great heights in the field you're in.

1222 (12:22)

Ascended Masters and other specialist guides are teaching you or sending you very special information to create something that may change the world significantly. Whether you patent a new idea, change a significant child's understanding of a concept, write a blog post about climate change solutions... whatever it is has been divinely timed and you are the one chosen to help in some way. Small or big, your contribution is part of your life path on Earth. Enjoy the special knowledge you'll receive and share it as you'll be guided.

13

You angels are sending you the message that something unusual is going to happen, but you needn't be alarmed.

This is a number of the individual, the odd one out. While you may feel this way about yourself, your angels and guides wish you to use that feeling to create something unique. This will help bring unity to certain spheres in your life and to help others who feel the same as you do!

1313 (13:13)

You'll be appreciated for your individuality, leadership, and or creativity. Your angels and guides are letting you know that any praise you hear at this time is sincere and out of genuine regard for your personality, ideas, or creative flair. Take these compliments as they're intended.

You may meet or encounter someone online who inspires you as much as you inspire them! For some, this could be your life partner or twin flame. You are very much the same and very much different. This will lead to fascination and creativity. You understand each other perfectly when it comes to working together on a creative or problem-solving project.

1414 (14:14)

Your celestial team is conveying that all your hard work is about to pay off. Keep the faith, keep up the pace, keep the good vibes going!

With 1414 seen often, it's no longer a case of "I think I can," but "I know I can!" You angels would like you to have this chant foremost in your mind.

For singles, it's a harbinger that love isn't far off, one that will be because of the foundations you're laying for your future, or a recent decision you've just made. Don't be surprised to see various twos and sequences of twos and 6s following to confirm this message!

1515 (15:15)

Along with other category meanings of 1515, on a personal level, it conveys, "It's time to walk your talk. Authenticity is crucial at this time, particularly in communication." Your heavenly team wants you to know that you may experience some tests and challenges to prove your authenticity. You may also be hyper-aware of hypocritical and hypocritical reasoning. Your personal filters to the world and people around you are growing more powerful. You may see this angel number often on social media.

1616 (16:16)

With 1616, your angels and guides are preparing you for a decision you have to make. This decision could be seen as a choice between a new beginning or an old love; a big change, or staying in your comfort zone. It could also be a choice between your needs and your family's needs. It won't be an easy decision for you so 1616 will mark little bits of information that will help you reach the healthiest decision for you!

1618 (16:18)

You may be more familiar with it as *Phi*, 1.618, or the Golden Ratio—the underlying natural ratio found in uncountable things from flowers to human biology to the solar system. When you see 1618, harmony and accuracy are important to your work. Through this message, your angels are encouraging and aiding your creative work.

Your celestial team would also like you to look deeper into the mysteries and synchronicities around you. You may begin to see underlying patterns and appreciate the underlying elegant simplicities of even the most complex creations. They assure you that the beauty and intricacies of nature and life will be revealed to you now.

1707 (17:07)

It's a countdown! Your celestial team are excited about the personal growth you've been through, your following of your wisdom, and your embracing of changes. Through 1707, they're letting you know that the countdown to the change you've been working toward in your finances or love is almost at an end! The time is right about now!

1717 (17:17)

Your heavenly team sends the message that you're doing great and will be doing even better! Your independence is growing, your reputation is elevated, and others may seek you out for your wisdom, work ethic, or even out-the-box thinking. You're embodying practicality and spirituality in a remarkable way. People are remarking on your authenticity, too! Expect to be in demand!

1808 (18:08)

The message from your guides says: "This ending is significant as it's empowering you and granting you success such as you've never conceived. Don't lament any losses at this time. You're much more powerful and creative now than you've ever been before. What you create next will be sustainable and solid." It's a great time to begin building passive income!

1818 (18:18)

This angel number carries a message about something needing to end. There may be a blockage or a contract (soul or other) that needs to be completed or dissolved before this cycle can close and the new beginning properly arrives. Until then, the cycle will keep bringing you up to a point, then taking you back to the start again as you keep waiting on your new beginning. This can be hugely frustrating. Look to other signs as to what's causing the cycle to repeat. You may need to see the contract through, renegotiate, or break the contract in the right way in order to release the situation and end the cycle.

Through 1818, your celestial team may send you a message about changes in your health or a loved one. A new treatment may be used, or a doctor changed. If the health issue is mysterious, an unusual test may give a definite diagnosis. Be open to new treatments and tests, and know that your angels and guides are beside you and your loved ones at this time.

1919 (19:19)

Through 1919, your angels want you to know that your good karma is at play. Your compassion and goodwill are returned. Someone whom you may have helped out in the past remembers and returns the favor. This situation will dissolve the karma between you.

For some, any decisions you made around the time you saw 1616 are now being acted upon, changing your life and others around you.

1919 also brings the message that you're going to quick bursts of personal evolution. Life is sure to be intensely exciting while you learn massive amounts about yourself, what you truly want from life, and about the people around you. It's a good time to stay out of the collective if you're a lightworker.

1333 (13:33)

You can accomplish something amazing at this time! Your angels and guides along with the ascended masters are excited to work with you on something special. Through your special skills be it creative work, culinary, literary, or healing; they're all working with you to accomplish a joint project. This project will fulfill you, part of your life's purpose, and uplift the community or world in a meaningful way. Connect with your angels and guides every morning (lighting a candle is good) and see what you can achieve together!

1555 (15:55)

You're in charge of the change in your life with 1555! Your heavenly team is waiting for your cue for your next spiritual and life's adventure. What do you want to experience next? The time is perfect to follow your heart, or even a whim, with the angels supporting you and your ideas. It's the perfect time to vision board, write letters of intent, and co-create with others. Your manifesting powers are high.

1999

Through 1999, your celestial team is sending you a caution. A new beginning is about to start, but you're in danger of repeating a karmic cycle if you don't work on the issue you were meant to deal with over this time. It's time to do the work, understand what needs to be done to release the karma so you can begin the new cycle light and free of past baggage and karma. You may want to do a de-cording and disconnecting ceremony.

1999 may also signal a party! You may be graduating or celebrating a very special time with a group or your family. There are new beginnings for or with everyone. Identities may change (marriage or careers), and there's lots of excitement and anticipation in the air. There's uncertainty, too, but your guides agree that the optimism in the air is well placed! Enjoy yourself and carry the high vibrations far into this new beginning!

2020 (20:20)

2020 holds a few messages from your heavenly team. It could signal their joy at your merging two aspects of yourself: masculine and feminine, or creative and logical, so you have more balance in your life and expression.

Another message may be that you've healed an old hurt or released a childhood programming that was causing a block in love or self-love. You'll now find it easier to find love, express love, and enjoy your relationships. Those singles who were attracting only frogs may now find their perfect prince or princesses!

Through 2020, your guides and angels may also be signaling that your vision is true. You may begin experiencing clairvoyance for the first time or have this ability enhanced. Follow your intuition and ensure you ground yourself often.

2112 (21:12)

You may be about to make a backstep and almost immediately move forward again. For some, it's advice that dance or other rhythmic movement would be great for you at this time.

There's a convergence from opposite spheres that's going to introduce a new partnership. This partnership or collaboration is going to bring an expansiveness and creativity that you'll love. Be open to working with and meeting with people from all walks of life.

2121 (21:21)

You are in harmony with all aspects of yourself. This balance brings you inner peace, greater emotional stability, and creativity. You'll sleep better, rest deeply even during short breaks, and be very effective and productive in your work.

Through 2121, your guides are communicating, "If you try out a new routine now, it will work very well for you! Be consistent to get the most out of your new routines, and don't be afraid to experiment and tweak them further."

2222 (22:22)

Your angels are letting you know that all that you currently desire is within your grasp, but that it may take a little more time and effort to get it all than you expect. Your angels are encouraging you to keep going—to keep putting in the effort. They know what you're working towards is going to reward you so much more than you think!

With 22:22, you may not hold all the pieces for what you want to come to fruition: someone else's will is very relevant, the time is not right, or an external force will dictate some of the steps. Be patient. This doesn't mean you'll receive what you seek. Still, you need to take action now to avoid any delays when matters are more favorable.

2999

Redemption is the theme of 2999's message from the angels. If you feel you've wronged another or failed in some way, your heavenly team is letting you know that you can now redeem yourself. They are also asking you if you can forgive yourself at this time. It would help you and the situation heal immeasurably. Thereafter, it's time to forgive others and allow them to heal, too!

303 (3:03)

With this message, your angels may be answering your question: How can I earn more money? "It's time to rework an old project or to revamp your resume. There are creative opportunities available for your polished or adapted project."

Another message of 303 is: Seek calm and stillness. It's time to stop the battle and make peace with the parties involved as well as yourself.

321

When 321 appears, be happy. Your guides are letting you know the final stage of your manifesting is here! It's a literal countdown. Get ready to go!

Alternatively, 321 from your angels may be a sign that your love or business situation is reaching a turning point. One of you wants to expand, the other may want to strike out on their own or continue as things are. Love and compromise will see you through this period of turbulence.

For creative workers and gardeners, 321 comes to remind you that you need to submit your work or complete it before the season changes. You may lose an opportunity or not get around to achieving what you intended if you don't act now. What are you waiting for? It's time to get moving!

3999

Your generosity and compassion will end a karmic situation for others. Through your support of a community, individual, or a greater cause, your contribution in time, money, or support in other ways will end a long standing genetic or karmic cycle.

Your creativity and charm can also come to the aid of others at this time, making their lives more bearable, or alleviating a bad situation for them. It's time to do good, and spread the word so others can do good, too!

404

When 404 pops up, probably when you're surfing the net, your angels and guides are letting you know you hold half the solution you're looking for. It's time to build on what you know, add the intention to find what you're looking for, and allow your intuition to lead you to the other half of the solution. It may take some time. It may take some digging, but you're in a stable situation and it's safe to take the time and get this solution figured out successfully. It will ground you in your future mastery of the subject or situation.

404 may also carry the message that you're moving to a new position at work but not much will change. It may be a lateral promotion or one in name only. In terms of relationships, your guides may want you to know that your current relationship has greater potential than you thought! Give it some time and you may be surprised. You may already be with your perfect partner!

4999

You've done well in maintaining stability for so long, but now it's time for a change. Your angels are giving you the heads up that the pace is picking up and you'll need to make some changes to your routine. Ensure they're healthy changes!

Through 4999, your celestial team reminds you that you have all that you are your own pillar of strength. Your spiritual and personal foundations are solid because they're anchored in you. No matter the changes and challenges, you will still emerge with your solid foundation and retain all you've worked for.

5999

Your creative ideas are life-changing! When 5999 is displayed by your guides they're guiding you to follow your most creative and original ideas. These ideas can change your life in wonderful ways. Whether it's an innovation that reduces your water consumption, or an illustration to brighten up someone's living space, your ideas are bringing ease to others and can earn you extra income.

Sometimes 5999 can indicate a vast change in your life—a total makeover of yourself and your life that retains little of your old habits and looks. You may also become more active and have more energy than ever before in your life!

618 (6:18)

In trying to create harmony and fairness, you may have forgotten to include yourself in the equation. Don't shortchange yourself. It will lead to disharmony and an imbalance.

Through 618, your celestial team is reminding you of the golden ratio or divine proportion when doing your work. It could answer your question or help you solve a problem related to design, space, or even fairness.

161 or 618 may also be messages to put love first! If you've been giving your heart and soul to your career, it may be time to reapportion your time, giving more priority to love and family, and to beauty and calm in your daily routine. "Let Love Rule!" say the angels.

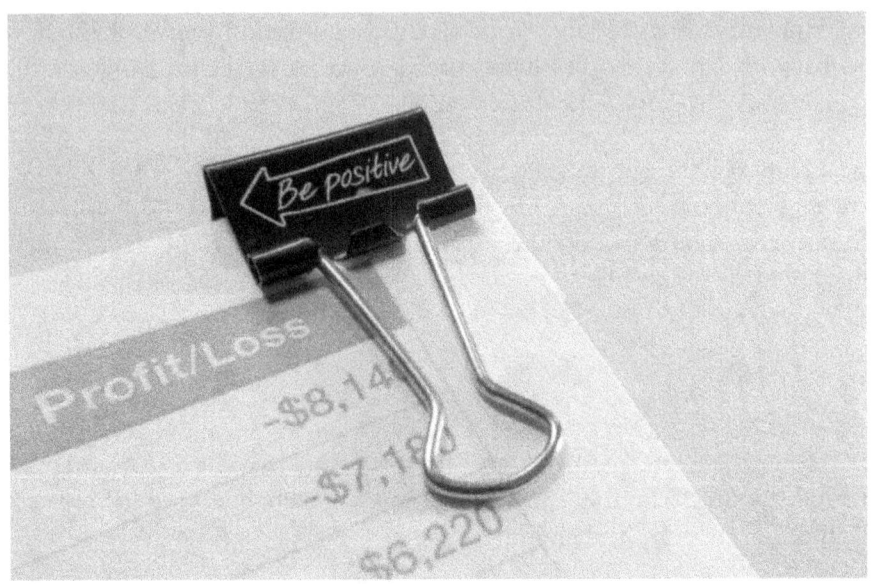

6220

When your angels and guides send you 6220, you'll soon be in demand for your spiritually uplifting manner or work. Your faith and optimism are inspiring and comforting to others at this time, and your words and voice carry compassion, love, and a conviction that resonates with most who hear you. It's a great time to give a speech, send a voice note, or sing a song. If you've always wanted to sing in a choir, this is the time!

6999

Your heavenly team would like to congratulate you on overcoming a great emotional burden or an addiction that took away from your love and relationships! Well done! Now enjoy your lighter energy and explore a new way of being with love, compassion, generosity. You may have lost some relationships, but it's possible for you to now find a new circle of friends while you heal relationships with family and precious friends. 6999 shows you that your true treasure in life is love and those who love you for you!

707 (7:07)

Your angels and guides want you to know that it's okay to take a break from your healing and esoteric studies. Sometimes career or love needs to take precedence for a little while. Your angels and guides will still be with you, and when you're ready, you can give more focus to your spiritual growth from where you left off.

707 may also be a message about integration. Your heavenly team is pleased that you've integrated your spiritual lessons and practices. New energy shifts and downloads will begin again after you're accustomed to all that you've integrated.

777

Known most widely as the jackpot or bingo number, 777 signals more than just a windfall or fantastic luck. Its links to mysticism and magic-working can be a sign that some of your guides may be Elementals or that you may be called to work with Elementals. It could indicate a deeper spiritual path has opened for you and that you may safely follow it.

777 is also the number that signals miracles. Sometimes, we aren't aware that we've witnessed a small miracle and the angels may remind you that your prayer was answered, so pay attention! Miracles are within reach at this time. Anything and everything will be possible. No wonder 777 is so often remarked on!

7999

Revelations about your past and past lives come to you now. You'll be aware of certain karmic cycles, why they began, and how to break them. Taking action with this knowledge now will help healings occur across time and space.

You've learned your karmic lessons and have integrated them successfully! You won't have to go through all that drama and trauma again! Your angels and guides are reminding you to apply your painfully gained wisdom and insight when needed to alleviate or prevent similar issues in the future. History does not have to repeat!

808

Your celestial team may send your 808 often when you're thinking about relocation. You may soon be relocating to an area you've always wanted to live in. Your angels confirm you'll feel blessed, understood, and around people who share the same outlook in life as you. You'll be in your true spiritual home!

When 808 appears regarding your business or career, you may choose to retire from your position and start a new business or begin a different career that you feel spiritually or passionately drawn to explore. Your heavenly team is supporting you all the way, and you'll be successful in your new ventures.

888

Some see this as a luckier number than 777. The triple eight brings assurance that abundance is here! Your guides may be announcing an abundance of good in your spiritual life, your love life, and especially your career. A windfall may suddenly come your way. While not many make a wish on this number, some Asian cultures revere it as the ultimate sign of success; so much so that they'll happily pay a premium for any phone number or address featuring the triple eight! When the angels send it to you, know you're very much blessed by the universe, especially financially and with good, helpful friends.

8585

When 8585 appears, your celestial team is concerned that you may not be dealing well with some significant changes in your life. Are you in denial over your age, your health, or the state of an important relationship? Or is your career or business in need of a reality check? If you're finding it hard to cope, ask for your heavenly team's help and matters will improve soon.

Another message from 8585 is a hint that a once-in-a-lifetime event is about to happen. You're in a good position to observe the event or participate. It's an event that could even be epic or in the history books. It's time to put your best feet forward and make the best of making history!

8999

If finances have been a worry, your angels are sending you 8999 to reassure you all is getting better! You've learned and integrated a soul lesson regarding abundance, money, and balance in your life. Now, you're at the end of this financially tough period, and with your lesson learned, you can safely depend on your own financial intuition and wisdom again. Life is getting better every day. Send gratitude to everyone involved and look forward to a healthier financial situation very soon!

Conclusion

Let's quickly review what you now know about the angelic communication we call angel numbers.

Angel numbers are any numbers that snag your attention in a remarkable way, then repeat themselves in random-seeming ways to draw your attention. These numbers carry messages from your celestial helper team (angels, guides, ancestors, lost loved ones) to guide you through difficulties and help you on your soul's evolution. Common and popular angel numbers often have repeating or mirroring digits, recur often, and grow in meaning the more familiar you become with them. Sometimes, angel numbers may be a repeating sequence or progression of numbers, too. For example, you may see 11, 22, 33 in quick succession, then 1234 sporadically over the next day or two. The sequence 1234 is brought to your attention and contains your angel message. You've also learned that a series of progressive angel numbers like 1010, 1111, 1212, 1313, signal a massive life change is on its way and that your angels and guides are preparing you for that transition. If the progression is reversed—1010, 901, 801, 701—you have a countdown to a major event or change in your life! Don't stress, your celestial team is working to make it all a seamless and happy time for you!

Sometimes angel numbers may follow you from the start to end of a situation, other times they may make only a brief appearance to alert you to a challenge or confirm what you already intuitively know.

Much like communicating with friends, the more you notice angel numbers, the stronger your communications with your guides and angels become.

You're now familiar with the core number meanings based on numerology, general interpretations of common angel numbers, interpretations of specific angel numbers in love, twin flame relationships, change, grief and grieving, messages from lost loved ones, and friendships.

Best of all, you now have the means to quickly decode almost any angel number you see. You have your core number meanings, your intuition, the general and category interpretations of commonly seen angel numbers, and you also have the internet as a further reference for additional meanings and alternate interpretations. Remember, your intuition is the *best* guide you have to help you discern which interpretation applies to you for that particular sighting. If you're still uncertain about the message of an angel number, ask for clarification and your guides will send you additional signs or numbers with similar messages so you have a reinforced, unmistakable message!

What It Means if You Stop Seeing Angel Numbers

If you stop seeing angel numbers or spot them with less frequency, it doesn't mean your angels and guides have deserted you. There could be a few reasons why you aren't as aware of these angel communications.

You could be in a low-energy (not frequency) state stemming from ill-health or exhaustion, caught up in the complexities of a work project, or while being an earth angel to someone else who constantly needs your help at this time. Your mind is too distracted or hyper-focused on other details.

Another reason—a very good reason—you may not see angel numbers for a while is that you've reached a higher level of consciousness and you've learned your life lessons for the time being. Your spiritual state is stable and content. It's like having your spiritual training wheels taken off because you're doing wonderfully well without any other help. You're in your sovereign power. When your next burst of spiritual evolution begins or you move out of this state of balance for any reason (prolonged ill health, job stress, heartache) the angel numbers will be back with messages of love and support when you're ready to receive them again.

Keeping a Journal

So many angel numbers with so many meanings! It's easy to be overwhelmed and become confused as to which meaning applies to you at present. This is where keeping track of angel numbers can be useful. You can start to identify the themes of the messages your angels and guides are sending you, allowing your interpretations to become more personalized over time. For example, seeing a progression of numbers such as 1234 or 3456 every time you feel you're failing is their way of letting you know you're progressing even if you can't see it just yet. Or if you see 11:11 and 11:22 every time you enter the mall, you may meet your twin flame, future life partner, or spiritual guide during one of your future visits to that mall.

In your journal or record of angel numbers, you may also want to note any intuitive messages you receive or any of your own personal decodings and meanings for that particular number. Many times, the standard meaning of a message or angelic sign may serve as the starting point for you to explore and understand your personal messages so that the messages grow ever more specific to your life and situations.

Don't forget to jot down the angel numbers you see in your dreams and meditations, too! Add any impressions, colors, people, symbols, and feelings you had at the time, as well. These details will add to your knowledge and further help you see how your angelic team tailors their messages especially for you. For example, if you see 888 in green, it may be a message about your finances or abundance, while an 888 in red or orange may be referring to your twin flame relationship.

I also suggest going through your angel number journal once in a while, and if you're still confused about a message or significance of a number, that you do a short meditation asking your guides to explain the significance of that number to you personally. It may hold a deeper meaning for you than most other angel numbers.

You can note your angel numbers in a journal, diary, or even your daily planner. Each format has a different approach in teaching you more about communicating with your angels.

The journal is great if you want to add all those details about the color of the number, the environment, and your whole experience at the time of receiving the number. These journal notes are the best when you're beginning or continuing your spiritual journey in a focused way, are at any stage of your twin flame journey, if you're in the process of grieving, or if you're looking to make a big change in your life even if you don't what that change might look like yet. All the details you record will spark off other avenues for you to explore and heal during your journeys. You may want to consider using a visual journal or sketchbook journal to add the colors, small sketches, or even a photo of the number or other significant sign spotted at the time. Updating this journal could be part of your spiritual work each day or week.

The diary method is best if you don't have a lot of time to keep a journal but still want to note as many significant details and meanings that struck you as relevant. You can use lists and abbreviations to note the theme of the angel number and other information.

The daily planner or calendar is a great way to keep track of angel numbers you're seeing if you're super busy. At a glance, you can track the frequency of which numbers are sent to you at which times and around which activities in your day.

Naturally, there's no reason you can't use a combination of the three methods to understand and decode your personal messages from angel numbers.

***

Thank you for journeying this far with me through angel numbers. I hope that you continue exploring the meaning of angel numbers and benefit from their celestial insight and guidance through each new situation you may experience. Let us give gratitude to our heavenly team for always looking out for our best interests.

Blessings and love to you and your celestial team,

Dawn

References

1 Angel Number—meaning and symbolism. (n.d.). Angelnumber.org. Retrieved December 26, 2021, from https://angelnumber.org/1-angel-number-meaning-and-symbolism/

Angel Number 222 meaning—relationship & love. (n.d.). Abundancenolimits.com; Abundance No Limits. Retrieved December 26, 2021, from https://www.abundancenolimits.com/222-meaning-relationship/

Angel Number 1414 meaning—achieving peace and joy—SunSigns.org. (2021, March 10). Sun Signs; Sun Signs. https://www.sunsigns.org/angel-number-1414-meaning/

Angel Number 6666 meaning: Your heart is full of love and compassion—About Spiritual. (n.d.). Aboutspiritual.com; About Spiritual. Retrieved December 26, 2021, from https://aboutspiritual.com/angel-number-6666-meaning/

Angel Numbers—What does number 0 to 999 mean. (n.d.). Angelnumbers.com; Angel Numbers.com. Retrieved January 4, 2022, from https://angel-numbers.com

Blakley, L. (2021, March 10). *Noticing 404? The amazing spiritual messages of Angel Number 404.* Subconsciousservant.com. https://subconsciousservant.com/404-angel-number/

Coffman, C. J. (1928). *Manual of the enumeration (online).* The Enumeration. https://www.gutenberg.org/files/35998/35998-h/35998-h.htm

Crawford, B. (2019, March 30). *Angel Numbers meanings and significance—A complete guide.* ZodiacSigns-Horoscope.com. https://www.zodiacsigns-horoscope.com/angel-numbers/angel-numbers-meanings/

Eason, C. (1998). *The complete book of divination : how to use the most popular methods of fortune telling.* Piatkus.

Eugene. (2017, November 13). *Angel Number 9.* Angel Numbers | Zodiac | Astrology | Tarot. https://thesecretofthetarot.com/angel-number-9/

Eugene. (2018, March 1). *Angel Number 101.* Angel Numbers | Zodiac | Astrology | Tarot. https://thesecretofthetarot.com/angel-number-101/

Eugene. (2019, August 15). *Angel Numbers | Zodiac | Tarot.* Angel Numbers | Zodiac | Astrology | Tarot. https://thesecretofthetarot.com

Fey, T. (2021, November 21). *Which angel numbers really symbolize love? An epic guide.* Love Connection; Digital Spirit Group LLP. https://loveconnection.org/angel-numbers-in-love/

Harris, K. (2021, January 30). *Angel Number 44 meaning & spiritual symbolism.* YourTango. https://www.yourtango.com/2020333564/spiritual-meaning-44

HiddenNumerology. (2020, October 17). *Angel number 1515 and the meanings of 1515.* Hidden Numberology.com; Hidden Numerology. https://hiddennumerology.com/angel-number-1515/

Hurst, K. (2016, July 26). *Why do I keep seeing 11:11, 9:11, or 21:21 everywhere?* The Law of Attraction. https://www.thelawofattraction.com/keep-seeing-numbers-1111-911-2121-everywhere-means-2/

Hurst, K. (2017, May 23). *Numerology Report: The secret meaning of numbers 0 to 9*. The Law of Attraction; Law of Attraction by Greater Minds. https://www.thelawofattraction.com/meanings-numbers-0-9/

Jones, W. (2021, September 21). *15 Twin Flame reunion numbers you should look out for*. PsychicBlaze.com; Walter Jones. https://psychicblaze.com/twin-flame-reunion-numbers/

Kumar, V. (2020, April 25). *Number sequences and what it means in twin flame journey*. TwinFlameUnion717.com. https://twinflameunion717.com/number-sequences-and-what-it-means-in-twin-flame-journey/

Master Number 33. (n.d.). GaneshaSpeaks; Pundit Ventures Private Limited. Retrieved January 4, 2022, from https://www.ganeshaspeaks.com/numerology/master-numbers/number-33/

Michaels, S. (2021, October 30). *Hidden Numerology authors*. Hiddennumerology.com. https://hiddennumerology.com/about-us/

Miller, K. (2021, February 4). *What does 303 mean?* The Word Counter. https://thewordcounter.com/meaning-of-303/

MindYourBodySoul, A. (2020, January 29). *Angel Number 8 meaning: Why you keep seeing it?* Mind Your Body Soul. https://www.mindyourbodysoul.com/angel-number-8/

MindYourBodySoul, A. (2021, December 14). *88 Angel Number: Meaning and symbolism*. Mind Your Body Soul. https://www.mindyourbodysoul.com/88-angel-number-meaning-and-symbolism/

Nag, G. (2020, January 9). *What is so special about the number 1.61803?* Medium. https://medium.com/@gautamnag279/what-is-so-special-about-the-number-1-61803-7e0bbc0e89e2

Nast, C. (2021, December 24). *Everything you need to know about angel numbers.* Allure; Conde Nast. https://www.allure.com/story/what-are-angel-numbers

Numerology, H. D. and W. (n.d.). *Numerology Master Number 33 | worldnumerology.com.* www.worldnumerology.com. Retrieved January 4, 2022, from https://www.worldnumerology.com/numerology-master-numbers/master-number-33/

Numerology.com Staff. (n.d.). *Angel Numbers: Repeating number sequences in numerology.* www.numerology.com; Zappallas USA. Retrieved December 26, 2021, from https://www.numerology.com/articles/about-numerology/angel-number-meanings/

Padre. (2017, October 10). *Angel Numbers—The Complete Online Guide for Angel Numbers.* https://www.guardian-Angel-Reading.com; Sesam Ltd. https://www.guardian-angel-reading.com/blog-of-the-angels/angel-numbers/

Rosario, B. (2020, August 25). *8 Angel Number twin flame reunion, love, meaning and luck.* My Today's Horoscope. https://mytodayshoroscope.com/angel-number-8/

Smith, L. (2020, February 14). *Angel Number 4999 meaning—Take the right path in life—SunSigns.org.* Sun Signs. https://www.sunsigns.org/angel-number-4999-meaning/

Smith, L. (2021, January 30). *Angel Numbers 0000, 1111, 2222, 3333, 4444, 5555, 6666, 7777, 8888, 9999: Meanings and symbolism—SunSigns.org.* Sun Signs. https://www.sunsigns.org/angel-numbers-0000-1111-2222-3333-4444-5555-6666-7777-8888-9999-meanings-and-symbolism/

Twin Flame Numbers: Sequences and patterns—Pure Twin Flames. (n.d.). PureTwinFlames.com; Danielle, Pure Twin Flames. Retrieved December 29, 2021, from https://puretwinflames.com/twin-flame-numbers/

Victoria Barnish. (2020, December 7). *Can angel numbers be two digits? Numerology Column.* https://numerologycolumn.com/can-angel-numbers-be-two-digits/

Which Angel Numbers signal that change is about to happen? –Takanta: Numerology, Angel Numbers, Pregnancy, Beauty. (n.d.). Takanta.com. Retrieved January 5, 2022, from https://takanta.com/angel-numbers-for-change

Whitaker, C. (2020, July 30). *1717 Angel Number twin flame reunion, love, meaning and luck.* My Today's Horoscope. https://mytodayshoroscope.com/angel-number-1717-meaning-love-reunion-and-unrequited-love-efforts-are-fruitful-luck-is-delivered/

Why you keep seeing multiple different Angel Numbers? (n.d.). Abundancenolimits.com; Abundance No Limits. Retrieved January 5, 2022, from https://www.abundancenolimits.com/seeing-multiple-different-angel-numbers/

Images

AnnaER. (2013). *House number 44.* In Pixabay. https://pixabay.com/photos/house-number-number-pay-digits-193789/

Ayrton, A. (2021). *Person on Weight Scales 1166.* In Pexels. https://www.pexels.com/photo/crop-person-on-weight-scales-6550832/

Birjoveanu, F. (2018). *House number 77.* In Pixabay. https://pixabay.com/photos/number-house-number-sign-blue-3749989/

Блажин, A. (2021). *Dirt bike with number 33.* In Pexels. https://www.pexels.com/photo/number-on-the-side-of-a-dirt-bike-10137438/

Brown, M. (2015). *Tennis 5 sets 5000*. In Pexels. https://www.pexels.com/photo/5-sets-won-0-sets-won-0-0-scoring-board-899318/

Chaensel. (2014). *Room 404*. In Pixabay. https://pixabay.com/photos/hotel-hotel-room-room-number-310225/

Cottonbro. (2020). *Number plate Washington 85858*. In Pexels. https://www.pexels.com/photo/plate-number-near-the-clear-glass-5599596/

Fietzfotos. (2021). *Wooden 13*. In Pixabay. https://pixabay.com/photos/number-thirteen-wooden-sign-shield-5979491/

Fox. (2019). *Digital readout 2353*. In Pexels. https://www.pexels.com/photo/white-digital-desk-clock-2046808/

Marco, P. (n.d.). *111*. In Pixabay. https://pixabay.com/photos/number-number-code-1932106/

Media, K. (2021). *Paper Clip 6220*. In Pexels. https://www.pexels.com/photo/marketing-desk-office-writing-7054383/

Nossing, E. (2017). *Old garage 22*. In Pixabay. https://pixabay.com/photos/old-number-garage-historical-2265967/

Pilger, K. (2019). *Aircraft A321*. In Pexels. https://www.pexels.com/photo/person-sitting-inside-airliner-seat-2276704/

Pixabay. (2017). *American Number Plates Art*. In Pexels. https://www.pexels.com/photo/american-number-plates-art-conceptual-creativity-533669/

Qian, A. (2019). *Flat Screen Monitor 1221*. In Pexels. https://www.pexels.com/photo/flat-screen-monitor-turned-on-in-office-2343475/

Shevtsova, D. (2018). *Tile 922*. In Pexels. https://www.pexels.com/photo/922-tile-1580332/

Tan, Y. H. (2021). *Blue Building 839*. In Pexels. https://www.pexels.com/photo/green-and-white-number-8-9144380/

Tarazevich, A. (2021). *Tile 69* [Pexels]. https://www.pexels.com/photo/a-tiles-with-number-6900686/

Vaitkevich, N. (2020). *Cherries on white 9*. In Pexels. https://www.pexels.com/photo/red-cherries-on-white-surface-4772870/

Winstead, T. (2021). *Dried herb leaves 60*. In Pexels. https://www.pexels.com/photo/dried-leaves-on-the-table-7111168/

www.ingramcontent.com/pod-product-compliance
Lightning Source LLC
Chambersburg PA
CBHW072336300426
44109CB00042B/1631